Stabilization Policy in an Exchange Rate Union

Contributions to Economics

Albrecht Ritschl
Prices and Production
- Elements of a System - Theoretic Perspective -
1989. 159pp. Softcover DM 59,-
ISBN 3-7908-0429-0

Arnulf Grübler
The Rise and Fall of Infrastructures
- Dynamics of Evolution and Technological Change in Transport -
1990. 305pp. Softcover DM 85,-
ISBN 3-7908-0479-7

Peter R. Haiss
Cultural Influences on Strategic Planning
1990. 188pp. Softcover DM 65,-
ISBN 3-7908-0481-9

Manfred Kremer/Marion Weber (Eds.)
Transforming Economic Systems: The Case of Poland
1992. 179pp. Softcover DM 69,-
ISBN 3-7908-91415-3

Marcel F. van Marion
Liberal Trade and Japan
1993. 298pp. Softcover DM 90,-
ISBN 3-7908-0699-4

Michael Carlberg
Open Economy Dynamics
1993. 203 pp. Softcover DM 75,-
ISBN 3-7908-0708-7

Hans Schneeweiß/
Klaus F. Zimmermann (Eds.)
Studies in Applied Econometrics
1993. 238 pp. Softcover DM 85,-
ISBN 3-7908-0716-8

Gerhard Gehrig/Wladyslaw Welfe (Eds.)
Economies in Transition
1993. 292 pp. Softcover DM 90,-
ISBN 3-7908-0721-4

Alfred Franz/Carsten Stahmer (Eds)
Approaches to Environmental Accounting
1993. 542 pp. Softcover DM 178,-
ISBN 3-7908-0719-2

János Gács / Georg Winckler (Eds.)
International Trade and Restructuring in Eastern Europe
1994. 343 pp. Softcover DM 98,-
ISBN 3-7908-0759-1

Christoph M. Schneider
Research and Development Management: From the Soviet Union to Russia
1994. 253 pp. Softcover DM 85,-
ISBN 3-7908-0757-5

Valeria De Bonis

Stabilization Policy in an Exchange Rate Union

Transmission, Coordination and Influence on the Union Cohesion

With 56 Figures

Physica-Verlag
A Springer-Verlag Company

Series Editor
Werner A. Müller
Peter Schuster

Author
Dr. Valeria De Bonis
University of Rome „La Sapienza"
Institute of Economics and Finance
Piazzale Aldo Moro, 5
I-00185 Rome, Italy

ISBN 978-3-7908-0789-9 ISBN 978-3-642-51526-2 (eBook)
DOI 10.1007/978-3-642-51526-2

Die Deutsche Bibliothek - CIP-Einheitsaufnahme
De Bonis, Valeria:
Stabilization policy in an exchange rate union : transmission, coordination, and influence on the union cohesion / Valeria De Bonis. - Heidelberg : Physica-Verl., 1994
(Contributions to economics)

88/2202-543210 – Printed on acid-free paper

PREFACE

The treaty of Maastricht envisages the full economic and monetary union in Europe. With increasing real and monetary integration policy decisions in individual member countries tend to have a growing impact on the other member countries of the European Community.

Against this background the following study analyses within a unified theoretical framework the impact of monetary and fiscal policy pursued by one country on its own macroeconomic performance as well as on those of the other member countries and of the rest of the world. The analysis contrasts the cases of a small and a large European union relative to the rest of the world and distinguishes very clearly between the short-run, the medium-run and the long-run effects. Based on this the consequences for union cohesion and the scope for policy coordination are discussed. Since the analytical framework is defined by a three country model many results from the traditional policy coordination literature which relies on two country models are qualified. In contrasts to most previous research in this area particular attention is paid to the implications of asymmetries between the EC member countries. Furthermore, the structural parameters are in some instances not taken as given but as responsive to the integration process. In this context numerous links to the traditional literature on optimal currency areas are established and interesting implications for union cohesion during the transition are derived.

The study reflects the state of the art of modelling currency unions and explores especially from the policy perspective useful directions of research. It will be a useful reference for all those concerned with the theoretical analysis of currency unions and with European integration.

Prof. Dr. Manfred Willms, University of Kiel

TABLE OF CONTENTS

CHAPTER III: MONETARY AND FISCAL POLICY IN A "SMALL" EXCHANGE RATE UNION - A STRATEGIC ANALYSIS

CHAPTER IV: AN IS-LM-AS MODEL FOR A "BIG" EXCHANGE RATE UNION

CHAPTER V: MONETARY AND FISCAL POLICY IN A "BIG" EXCHANGE RATE UNION - A STRATEGIC ANALYSIS

INTRODUCTION

In which ways do macroeconomic policy changes in one country belonging to an exchange rate union affect its own macroeconomic performance, that of the other members and that of the countries extraneous to the union? Can the countries improve their performance by taking into account the reciprocal policy spillovers? How do the transmission and coordination of macroeconomic policy changes affect the exchange rate union cohesion?

These questions have been separately addressed by the literature on currency unification. The efficacy of stabilization policy is analysed mainly by the use of IS-LM models, with two countries linked by irrevocably fixed exchange rates and floating as a single block with respect to the rest of the world. The problem of policy coordination is tackled within the frame of the game theoretical approach, on the basis of two-country rational expectation models. The aspect of the convenience and conditions for existence of an exchange rate union traces back to the original literature on the optimality of a currency area and its Phillips curve developments, these also referring to a two-country world.

The object of the following chapters is to unify the treatment of these questions by developing the policy efficacy, policy coordination and union cohesion analyses on the basis of a unique model. This is an IS-LM-AS model with a third component, the rest of the world, beside the two countries members of the exchange rate union. The context is therefore different from that of the change from a regime of flexible to one of fixed exchange rates, as it is to be found in the two-country world models. As far as analytically feasible, the two member countries are not supposed to be "mirror images" of each other. This permits to treat the issue of the convenience for a country to be a member of an exchange rate union according to its economic characteristics with respect to the transmission and coordination of policy. Particular attention is given to the change in structural parameters deriving from the unification process and its repercussions on the cohesion question. The short-, medium- and long-run scenarios are contrasted and both the case of a small and that of a big exchange rate union are studied.

Chapter I presents an overview of the existing literature on currency unification, in particular that concerning the optimality criteria, the conditions for existence, the efficacy of economic policies as analysed by means of IS-LM models, the coordination of policies as studied for the case of the European Monetary System. In chapter II the model for the small union case is developed. It is an extended version of the Mundell-Fleming two-country model with the rest of the world as a third exogenous component. The efficacy and the transmission mechanisms of monetary and fiscal policy are analysed for the short run, the medium run and the long run, differentiated by the Phillips curve foundations of the aggregate supply curve. Conclusions are then drawn for the union cohesion from the transmission of the policy effects. Chapter III presents the game theoretical application of the model developed in chapter II. The results of the union member-countries' strategic behaviour in the conduction of monetary and fiscal policies are analysed with particular reference to the union cohesion and contrasted with those obtained in the two-country models.

In chapter IV the model for the big union case is developed: changes in the union variables affect those of the rest of the world, which are therefore considered endogenous. The complexity of the model, deriving from the high number of equations and endogenous variables, imposes the necessity of some simplification: the union member-countries are therefore considered to be mirror images and the issue of the union cohesion is tackled with respect to the reciprocal spillover effects with the rest of the world. The model is also used to study the effects of a change from a regime of internationally fixed to one of internationally flexible exchange rates. Chapter V illustrates the strategic implications of the model developed in chapter IV. The results are analysed with particular reference to the effects on the union cohesion of the cooperation with the rest of the world. The issue of the different scope for policy coordination under the regimes of internationally fixed and flexible exchange rates is also analysed.

I am grateful to Prof. Dr. Manfred Willms, whose stimulating advice has constantly accompanied my work, and to Prof. Dr. Hans-Werner Wohltmann for helpful suggestions and comments. This book is dedicated to Pietro and Maria Teresa.

CHAPTER I
THE STATE OF THE ART

Introduction

This chapter contains an exposition of the "state of the art" of the literature on exchange rate and monetary unions. Given the large amount of work on the topic, this illustration does not aim to be complete, but to offer some examples of the main issues tackled.

Initially, the original optimality criteria for single currency areas will be presented, together with the successive cost-benefit and Phillips curve approaches. This traditional stream has always combined the macro and microeconomic analysis of the problem, deriving the conditions for the opportunity of currency unification from the underlying system of economic interdependence between the countries considered.

These aspects have been studied separately by the more recent literature. The microeconomic ones have been analysed mostly outside the exchange rate/monetary union literature, especially in the context of the role of uncertainty in the reallocation of factors. The macroeconomic aspects, as it will be shown, have been developed either through models extending the traditional two-country IS-LM analysis to a situation where the "rest of the world" is also present beside the union members, or through game theoretical analyses applying the issues introduced by the rational expectation literature.

1. The optimality criteria

Mundell (1961), addressing the question of what constitutes an optimum currency area, showed, in a model with two countries and rigid nominal wages, that the opportunity of forming a single currency area depends on the degree of factor mobility between the regions concerned.

The difference in the adjustment process between a single currency area and one with different currencies is illustrated as follows: given two regions, A and B, and a shift of the demand for goods from those produced in the second one towards those produced in the first one, unemployment in B together with inflationary pressure and balance of payment surplus in A will result.

With different currencies, if A's monetary authority reduces the supply of money in order to oppose inflation, the price level does not increase in this country and B bears the whole burden of unemployment. With a single currency, if an expansionary monetary policy is adopted in country B in order to avoid unemployment, there will be an increase in country A's price level. Unemployment and inflation cannot both be avoided.

The flexibility of the exchange rate cannot correct balance of payments imbalances between two *regions*, even if it will do so between two countries with *national currencies*.

In fact, if demand shifts from B's towards A's products, the consequent depreciation in B and appreciation in A correct the external imbalance stopping the tendency to unemployment in the first country and the inflationary pressure in the second one.

However, if there are two countries and two regions (East and West) not corresponding to the national boundaries, and demand shifts from eastern to western products, unemployment in the first region and inflationary pressure in the second one will result. Central banks should increase the supply of money to increase employment in the East, while they should reduce it to prevent inflation in the West.

In conclusion, flexible exchange rates are effective if based on regional currencies. Regions, in their turn, should be delimited on the basis of factor mobility. Flexible exchange rates are preferrable with low mobility. Under conditions of high mobility, instead, the demand shift from one region to the other one causes neither unemployment, since those who loose their jobs in the region hit by the recession can find a place in the richer one, nor balance of payments problems, since the factors movement replaces the goods one.

In other words, a high degree of labour mobility can substitute the flexibility of the exchange rate as an adjustment mechanism. Given the advantages deriving from the use of a single currency (see further), it is therefore preferable for countries between which factors mobility is high to form a single currency area.

Another criterion for the optimality of a single currency area, suggested by McKinnon (1963), is the *degree of openness*, measured by the importance of the sector producing tradables relative to that of the sector producing non tradables in the single regions. A high degree of opennes reduces the efficacy of the (nominal) exchange rate flexibility as a policy instrument. A depreciation would cause a change in the relative prices of domestic and foreign goods: the demand for exports and domestic demand for goods which are substitutes for the imported ones increases and therefore resources are shifted from the non tradables to the tradables sector. Being the former small, these movements will have such an inflationary effect that the comparative advantage gained by depreciation are eliminated.

Kenen (1969) proposed that economies with a high degree of product (and consumption) *diversification* should form a single currency area. These countries are characterized by a low degree of real exchange rate variability, because independent shocks hitting different economic sectors tend to cancel each other's effects. In other words, countries with a highly diversified production will also have diversified exports; if demand for some type of exported goods drops, there will be other goods for which export demand is very high and global export will tendentially be more stable than in the case of a country which concentrates production and exports in one sector. This means that the balance of payments of the former will be more stable and the need for exchange rate changes will be lower.

A criterion incorporating the above mentioned ones is that proposed by Vaubel (1978): in a currency area with fixed exchange rates, changes in the nominal exchange rates requires an adjustment in the national price levels. Since this is in contrast with one of the fundamental macroeconomic targets, price stability, only countries with small changes in the *real exchange rates* can form a single currency area. These tipically have similar preferences for price stability and productivity trends, apart from highly diversified goods and financial markets.

This criterion, moreover, comprehends the three above mentioned ones. First, factor mobility reduces unemployment in the backward areas, so that fewer attempts are made to lower the real wage in these regions through depreciation; moreover, "since high factor mobility implies high price elasticities of factor supply and ultimately high price elasticities of commodity supply, demand shifts will produce output rather than price effects so that real exchange-rate changes will be small [Vaubel (1978), p. 65]" . Second, high trade diversification reduces the size and probability of changes in the real exchange rate. Finally, the greater the openness of the economy, the smaller the availability of exchange rate illusion for real adjustment through nominal exchange rate changes.

These criteria have been used by Willms (1991) to address the question whether the twelve countries of the European Community are suitable for a monetary union. The answer that they deliver is ambiguous: while the degree of factor mobility is rather low, because of different language, cultural background and the like, the European countries present a high degree of openness and, at least some of them, of production and trade diversification.

Another approach present in the literature on optimum currency areas is the cost-benefit one, which is based on the singling out and the evaluation of the advantages and the disadvantages of joining a monetary union [see for instance Gandolfo (1986) and Bean (1992)].

The main benefits which have been specified are: 1) the reinforcing of the function of measure of value, medium of exchange and store of value of money; 2) the elimination of speculative capital flows; 3) the saving of foreign reserves (being these not necessary any more for the trade between the union member countries); 4) the sharing of the risk of economic crises; 5) the competion between fiscal systems; 6) the increase of the "bargaining" power of the member countries at the international level.

On the costs' side the following are shown: 1) the loss of autonomy in the conduction of monetary policy; 2) the loss of autonomy in the conduction of fiscal policy; 3) the deterioration of regional economies.

Three of these points seem particularly relevant.

a) On the side of the benefits, fixed exchange rates (and even more a single currency) favour trade and financial integration. Eichengreen (1990) has pointed out that in the period between the two World Wars the variability of the real exchange rates has increased together with that of the nominal exchange rates. An increasing variability of the exchange rate also means an increasing variability of relative prices, to the prejudice of international trade. Fixed exchange rates also favour financial integration, in terms of a higher capital mobility and a decreasing interest rate differential. The latter, in fact, is formed by the covered interest rate differential, the risk premium and the expected real depreciation (i. e. that part of the price increase not compensated by the currency depreciation). Fixed exchange rates reduce the differential acting on its last two components (the first one, instead, depends on the intensity of the controls on capital movements).

b) On the side of the costs there is the loss of autonomy in the conduction of monetary and fiscal policy. The loss of monetary autonomy derives from the locking of parities and perfect capital mobility. Apart from what set forth relatively to the macroeconomic objectives, two other disadvantages are represented by the loss of seigniorage revenues and the impossibility of substaining the financial system with money immissions, when it is in situations of high instability.

c) As for fiscal policy, the higher labour mobility induced by the integration process can make the imposition of higher taxes, limited to one country, more difficult, since the factors of production would emigrate towards the regions where the fiscal pressure is lower. The conclusion is that the impossibility of increasing taxes, together with the loss of the power of creating money, makes debt financing more irksome.

The literature on the optimality criteria and the weighing up of the costs and the benefits tackles the question of whether it is convenient or not for a country to join a monetary union, in other words which is the optimal size of the latter. A different, altough connected problem, is under which conditions countries already forming a monetary union can keep their exchange rates at the fixed parity, i. e. which are the conditions for the survival of the union.

2. Conditions for existence of a monetary union

De Grauwe (1975), with an approach tracing back to Fleming (1971) and Corden (1972), analyses the necessary conditions for a monetary union to exist with a two-country model focused on the inflation-unemployment trade-off expressed by the Phillips curve.

The first quadrant of Fig. 1 [taken from De Grauwe, 1975] shows the Phillips curve for country A; the second one the relation between the wage growth rate and the price growth rate - the intercept of the line indicates the productivity growth rate. The third and fourth quadrants represent the same relationships for country B. Let point *S* indicate the inflation-unemployment combination chosen by the monetary authority in country A, while that of country B chooses *T*. The rate of growth of the price level is higher in B than in A; therefore, the currency of the first country depreciates.

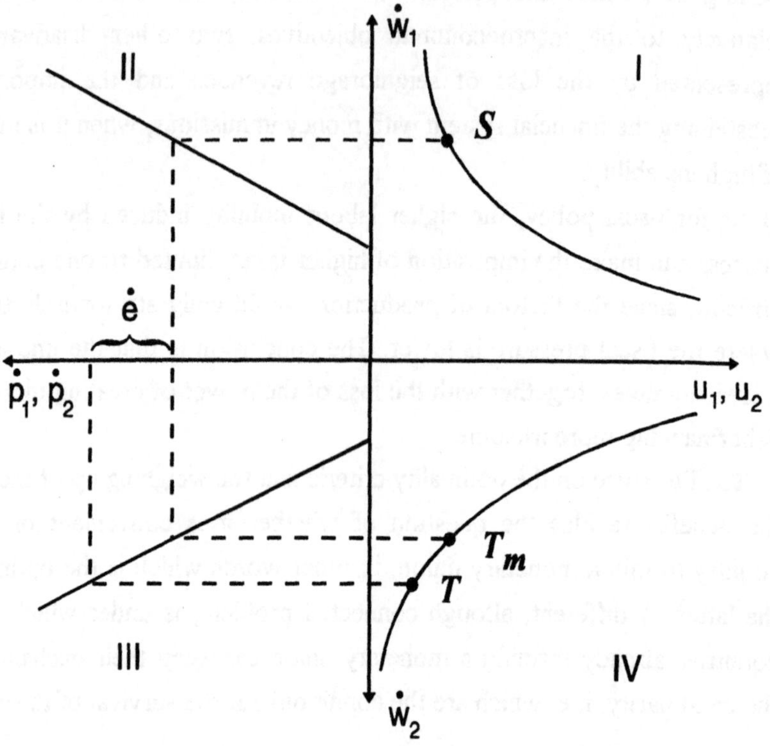

Fig. 1: The loss of monetary autonomy in an exchange rate union.

If the two countries want to form a monetary union, the exchange rate between their currencies must be locked at a fixed parity. This will be possible only if the combination of inflation and unemployment chosen by the two countries will be the same, as it happens, for instance, if A imposes its objectives to B. Belonging to a monetary union, therefore, involves the loss of the autonomy in the conduction of monetary policy. One can comment that this is anyhow not particularly relevant if, in an open economy, domestic inflation is calculated using the foreign currency - otherwise it would be necessary to assume that economic agents are subject to a sort of exchange rate "illusion".

This can be seen using the four-quadrant diagram of Fig. 2. Quadrant IV shows a Phillips curve, c, relating the unemployment rate u to the rate of change of wages $\dot{w}$ in one country. Quadrant III shows the relationship between $\dot{w}$ and the cost, i. e. price growth rate, $\dot{p}$ (line q), the intercept of the line, OQ, being the productivity growth rate. Quadrant II converts $\dot{p}$ into $\dot{p}-\dot{e}$, i. e. inflation measured in foreign currency, through line r, the intercept *E* being equal to the depreciation rate, $\dot{e}$. Finally, quadrant I shows the relationship between u and $\dot{p} - \dot{e}$: it is a Phillips curve with inflation measured in foreign currency (f).

Point *A* on the Phillips curve corresponds to point *D* on the wage-price passing function and to point *L* on the domestic currency measure-foreign currency measure of inflation one and therefore to point *H* on the Phillips curve with inflation measured in foreign currency.

If the authorities want to move from point *A* to point *B*, they will face an increase in wage and therefore price inflation. If inflation abroad does not change and the purchasing power assumption holds, this will involve a depreciation rate equal to the inflation differential. A depreciation causes a leftward shift of the r line to the new intercept OE'.

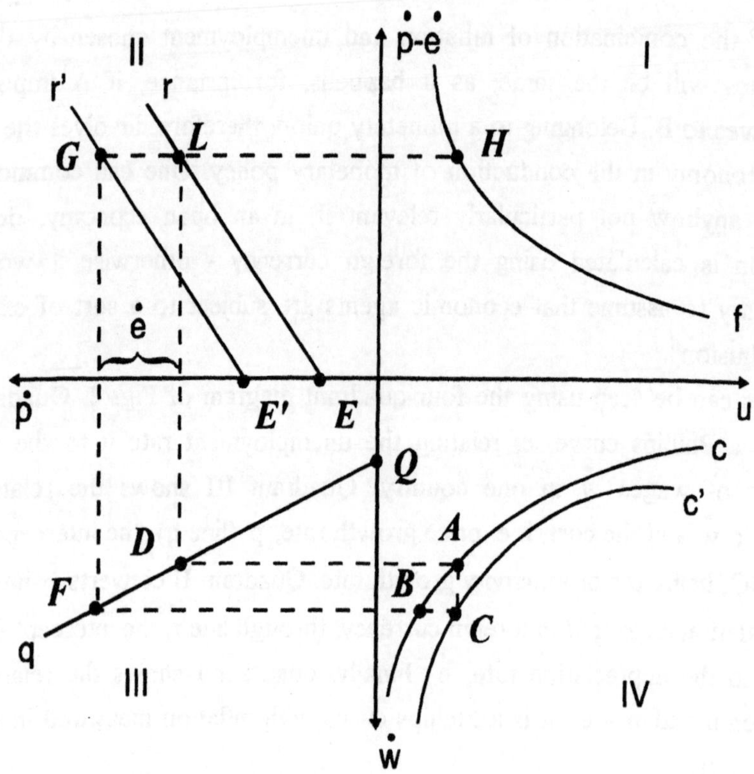

Fig. 2: The case of absence of exchange rate illusion.

The point on f, i. e. the Phillips curve with inflation measured in foreign currency, does not change. The new inflation-unemployment combination is shown by point *C*: the original Phillips curve, c, has shifted downward to c', since economic agents realize that the new rate of wage inflation, nominally higher than before, is the same if measured in foreign currency, and is therefore consistent with the previous unemployment level, shown by point *A*, and not with that indicated by *B* on the old curve.

Authorities, therefore, cannot "buy" less unemployment with a higher inflation rate in this case and moving to a monetary union does not involve any cost consequent to the loss of policy autonomy, since the latter is already ineffective under this respect.

However, as pointed out by Fleming, "The fact that the regions of an existing country could not hope to have separated exchange rates because of the impossibility of creating a regional money illusion, does not imply that countries of a similar size, where national money illusion persists, should not retain separate exchange rates. National currencies, unless thoroughly abused by inflation, have shown great powers of retaining their functions as means of exchange and standards of value for all domestic transactions, particularly the payment of wages. And while cost-of-living clauses in wage agreements are quite widespread, they seldom operate instantaneously or more than partially to offset the effect of exchange rate adjustments [Fleming, 1971, p. 247]".

In the case that monetary policy has no effect on employment - vertical Phillips curve - the condition for two countries to form a monetary union is that the rate of change of prices is the same in both of them. In this situation, which corresponds to the monetarist case, the only potential cost of currency unification is the effect that it may have on nominal magnitudes.

In the case of a shock shifting demand from the union member-country B to the union member-country A, once the nominal exchange rate is irrevocably fixed, real exchange rate changes may occur only through movements in the domestic price level (inflation in A and deflation in B).

As pointed out by Vaubel, "... nominal exchange-rate changes are likely to be a less costly way of producing real exchange-rate adjustment than movements of domestic price levels as long as the volume of domestic transactions exceeds the volume of transactions with other potential members of the currency area being contemplated. Even if the latter condition is not fullfilled, the fact that, on average, international transactors seem to be better equipped to cope with nominal exchange-rate changes than ordinary citizens are to cope with domestic price-level movements, may tip the balance in favour of exchange-rate flexibility [Vaubel, 1978, p. 3]".

In a monetarist world, therefore, national price level instability is the risk of currency unification and the Vaubel criterion, i. e. the need for real exchange rate changes between the member countries, offers an evaluation of the economic cost related to it. This is also an example of the connection between the optimality, costs and benefits and conditions for existence approaches to the problem of currency unification. Willms (1992) makes a cost-benefit analysis integrated with the optimality criteria and the Phillips curve approach, reaching the conclusion that "... negative Effekte sind für relative grosse Länder mit hoher Präferenz für Preisniveaustabilität zu erwarten", which derives from the McKinnon criterion and the Phillips curve approach for the monetarist case.

One definition of optimal currency area which can be derived from the above exposition is the following: an economic unit formed by regions symmetrically hit by the same shocks and between which labour and the other factors of production are highly mobile. In fact, if the regions undergo the same shocks, changes in relative prices do not become necessary. Moreover, should local unemployment pockets still remain, factor mobility would make them eliminable. One should finally not forget that, when dealing with factor mobility, freedom of circulation does not imply real mobility (abstracting from considerations on the desirability of it).

3. The change in structural parameters

The requirements which potential member-countries should meet cannot be evaluated with regard to their pre-union characteristics. In fact, these may be changed by the unification process itself and with them the evaluation of the optimality/survival conditions. The problem has been tackled with respect to the degree of factor mobility and inflation-unemployment trade-off. A study refferring to regional problems is to be found in Pace (1978).

a) Factor mobility

Factor mobility is not predetermined with respect to the choice of the exchange rate regime. One can, for instance, consider the choice of a labour supplier who has the possibility of emigrating from country A to country B. If the present discounted value of the flow of income in B is bigger than that in A, the agent is willing to emigrate.

However, the persistence of this positive differential is not certain. Bertola (1989) shows that the higher the uncertainty is, the greater the difference between the wage rates in the two countries must be to make the agent emigrate. These results are derived using a real option model with an exercise price. If the choice of the exchange rate regime affects the degree of uncertainty relative to the persistence of the differential between the flow of income in A and that in B, factor mobility is a variable endogenous to the system.

In the case of a change from a flexible to a fixed exchange rate regime, there are two factors to be considered: a) the variability of the nominal exchange rate is eliminated: this reduces uncertainty and therefore improves factor mobility; b) the way in which the variability of income is affected is not univocal.

As more widely shown later, these considerations can be linked to macroeconomic ones: flexible exchange rates, which act directly on competitivity and therefore on the IS curve, are a stabilizing mechanism in the case of shocks affecting the real sector of the economy; fixed exchange rates, which can be kept at the desired level by varying the stock of international reserves, are stabilizing when the shocks hit the LM curve. Only if this type of shocks is predominant, therefore, uncertainty is decreased when moving to a fixed exchange rate sytem.

In general, variability and uncertainty on the level of income influence factor mobility, which, in its turn, can act as an adjustment mechanism replacing the flexibility of the exchange rate.

b) The inflation-unemployment trade-off

The parameters underlying the inflation-unemployment trade-off may change because of the unification process. In particular, the trade-off between wage inflation and unemployment and the productivity growth rate may change.

As for the first aspect, one reason is the change in the bargaining positions of firms and trade-unions. If the price of the goods exported by a country increases, foreign demand for it goes down. This brings about a decrease in employment and in profits.

If the exchange rate is flexible, a depreciation may counteract the price increase. But if the exchange rate is irrevocably fixed, this mechanism is not available any more. Therefore, with fixed exchange rates, on the one hand enterpreneurs have a particular interest in obtaining low wage rate agreements with the unions; these, on the other hand, assuming that they care both for wage and employment, might fear that an increase in the wage rate would reduce the employment level and cause a loss of foreign markets, thus decreasing scale economies and therefore future productivity and real wage improvements.

This will particularly apply to countries with a large foreign sector. For instance, if country B of Fig. 1 is in this situation, shifting to a fixed exchange rate regime may cause its Phillips curve slope to change so that the unemployment rate corresponding to point *H* is now compatible with a fixed exchange rate with country A, as shown in Fig. 3.

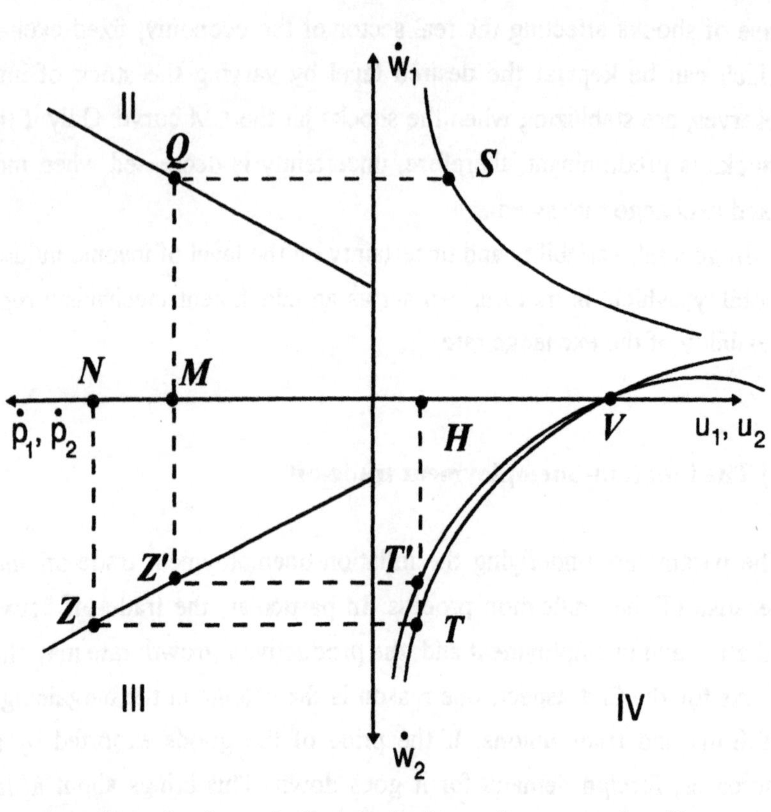

Fig. 3: The effect of a change in the inflation/unemployment trade-off.

As for the second aspect, the completion of an economic union, which a monetary union should facilitate by eliminating the exchange rate risk and relative transaction costs, should bring about an increase in productivity through higher efficiency and enlarged scale economies. This causes the wage-cost passing function to shift, since its intercept is a measure of the productivity growth rate. If country A enjoys a relatively higher increase in productivity or, to make the graph simpler, is the only one to experience it, its preferred unemployment-inflation combination, *S*, would become even less compatible with that chosen by country B, *T*, and the loss of monetary autonomy necessary to keep the exchange rate at the fixed parity even more relevant, as shown in Fig. 4.

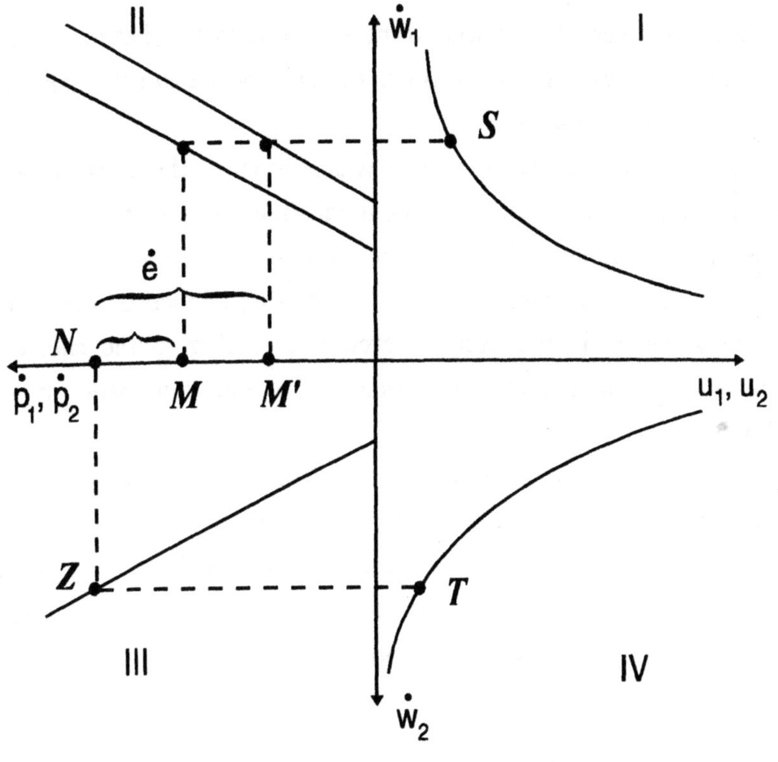

Fig. 4: The effect of a change in the productivity growth rate.

But which countries are more likely to experience a relatively higher increase in productivity once they join a monetary union? To be precise, these benefits derive from the economic unification process which accompanies the monetary one and accrue to regions rather than to countries. In general, it is agreed upon that "completion of the internal market represents a process that, whilst having a positive effect on the growth rate of the global ... economy, will nonetheless provoke an uneven distribution of these benefits amongst the various regions [Senn, 1992, p. 176]".

Moreover, the more developed regions are likely to be more favoured by the process. In fact, on the demand side, the price reduction due to the abolition of tariff barriers will benefit consumer with a wider and more rational choice; on the supply side, the agglomeration of production processes and the development of cooperative alliances will "... imply asymmetry in the relationships between the various firms - an asymmetry that presumably will reward the more developed regions and penalize those that are weaker and less autonomous [Senn, 1992, p. 176]".

As for the specific characteristics which enhance the competitivity of a region in exploiting the benefits of the unification process, these are mainly to be found in its centrality with respect to the core of the union, in the presence of sectors subject to deregulation and in the importance of the country to which they belong in the decision processes leading to the choice of the irrevocably fixed parities and the harmonization and coordination of national policies.

The examples of the changes in the degree of factor mobility and in the Phillips curve show how the analysis of the optimality/survival of a currency area should not be made with reference to the models and the parameters describing the economy prior to the unification, but to those referring to the (foreseen) changes introduced by the process itself.

4. The underlying models

The analysis of the optimality and the conditions of existence of a currency area has always combined the micro and macroeconomic aspects of the problem. As for the latter, the system of macroeconomic interdependence is usually derived from an IS-LM model, either in the "Keynesian" or in the "monetarist" version, describing the relationship between two countries linked by fixed exchange rates, as, for instance, in Mussa (1979). This traditional two-country model has been more recently extended to take into account the influence of the non-members on the union interdependence system.

Levin (1983), Sauernheimer (1984, 1991), Moutos/Scarth (1988), Feuerstein/Siebke (1990), Feuerstein (1992), Wohltmann (1993) and Thomsen (1992) analyse stabilization policy within a monetary union with IS-LM-AS type models. These elaborations can be generalized as follows.

The main aim is to take into account the characteristics of a monetary union, i. e. the fixing of parities between the members, the pooling of foreign reserves and the conduction of a common foreign exchange policy, together with a system of flexible exchange rates with the countries which do not belong to the union. To accomplish this, a three-component model is constructed, which allows for the analysis of the relationships between a union member-country, the rest of the union and the rest of the world.

This is achieved by a modification of the Mundell-Fleming model. A second equation, expressing the goods market equilibrium condition for the rest of the union, is added and the money market equilibrium condition, being one for the whole union, is represented by a unique LM curve equation. The rest of the world comes into the model with its exogenously fixed income level and interest rate, which are arguments of the model functions.

However, this model is analysed introducing simplifying hypotheses, such as the symmetry of the reaction functions of the union member countries. As a consequence of this, the microeconomic components of the problems relative to stabilization policy within a single currency area and the fundamental question of its optimality are not tackled.

When a flexible exchange rate with the rest of the world is assumed, it is shown that, in the short run, monetary policy has a positive effect on both union member countries, while fiscal policy is negatively transmitted; in the long run, monetary policy is ineffective and fiscal policy can be either positively or negatively transmitted. As for the fixed exchange rates case, the short run results are that monetary policy is ineffective while fiscal policy is positively transmitted.

Apart from the IS-LM context, other models are used in the literature to analyse macroeconomic interdependence between countries which have unified their currencies, in particular those underlying the game theoretical literature, illustrated in the following section.

5. The game theoretical approach

The rational expectations literature has introduced new issues in macroeconomic theory - policy neutrality debate, time consistency problem, international policy coordination, etc. - which have been applied also to the problem of currency unification, especially in the game theoretical models of the European Monetary System, among which one can choose those in Fratianni/von Hagen (1990) and Collins (1988) for illustration purposes.

Fratianni and von Hagen consider the EMS an instrument for implementing policy coordination in response to exogenous shocks, common to all the members of the system. The need for coordination derives from the spillover effects of monetary policy. For instance, given that the central banks of the member countries want to achieve price stability and a high employment rate, it can be shown that the single central bank can improve the trade-off between the two variables to the foreign partners' cost through real exchange rate movements induced by its own monetary policy.

In fact, if a productivity shock causes an upward pressure on the price level in country A, the central bank can reduce the money supply and counteract it at the cost of more unemployment. However, this operation will also induce an exchange rate appreciation: the consequent decrease in the price of imported goods will, in its turn, act as a force decreasing the general price level, but this time with no negative effect on employment. Instead, the relative price of the goods produced by A and imported by the other member of the system, B, will increase. The existence of spillover effects of the domestic monetary policy on the foreign price level explains why countries can improve their welfare by coordinating their policy choices.

Before giving an analytical description of the model, which goes back to the Canzoneri/Henderson (1988) one, one must recall the assumptions underlying it (some of which do not belong to the original model but are introduced here for the sake of simplification). The model is a two-country one. The two union members are equally sized and "mirror images" of each other; in particular, they have the same natural rate of output and average propensity to import (which is also equal to the marginal propensity). Moreover, capital mobility is absent, government spending is neutral and monetary authorities act on the basis of full information.

The variables (in logarithms) will be indicated by means of the following notation:

superscript * denotes foreign variables;
superscript ^ denotes deviations from full employment levels;
superscript $^{-}$ denotes full employment (= expected) values;
b = propensity to import;
e = nominal exchange rate;
m = money supply;
n = employment;
p = product price;
q = consumer price index;
s = real exchange rate;
w = nominal wage;
x = productivity disturbance;
y = output.

The model can then be simplified as follows:

(1) $$y = (1\text{-}a)n + x, \qquad 0 < a < 1,$$

(2) $$y^* = (1\text{-}a)n^* + x,$$

(3) $$w - p = -an + x,$$

(4) $$w^* - p^* = -an^* + x.$$

Equations (1) and (2) are the production functions; (3) and (4) say that labour is employed until its marginal product equals the real wage.

Wage setters choose a wage ($\overline{w}$) consistent with full employment at the announced level of the money supply (available in the absence of disturbancies). At this level of the real wage, all labour demanded is supplied. One thus has:

(5) $$w = \overline{w},$$

(6) $$w^* = \overline{w}^*.$$

The equilibrium condition for the market for the home good is the following:

(7) $$y = (1\text{-}b)y + by^* + (1/d)s, \qquad 0 < b < 1.$$

In the absence of capital mobility, equilibrium in the home goods market implies equilibrium also in the foreign goods one. The equivalent of (7) for the foreign country is therefore redundant and will not be considered. The real exchange rate is defined as:

(8) $$s = e + p^* - p.$$

The consumer price indices are:

(9) $$q = (1\text{-}b)p + b(e+p^*) = p + bs,$$

(10) $$q^* = b(p\text{-}e) + (1\text{-}b)p^* = p^* - bs.$$

The money market equilibrium conditions are:

(11) $$m = p + y,$$

(12) $$m^* = p^* + y^*.$$

The model will now be expressed in terms of deviations of the variables from their full employment (= expected) levels. From equations (3), (5) and (9) one gets:

(13) $$\hat{q} = a\hat{n} + b\hat{s} - x.$$

Similarly, for the foreign country:

(14) $$\hat{q}^* = a\hat{n}^* - b\hat{s} - x.$$

From equations (1), (2) and (7) one gets:

(15) $$0 = (1-b)(1-a)\hat{n} + b(1-a)\hat{n}^* + (1/d)\hat{s} + (1-b)x + bx.$$

From (1), (3) and (11) one obtains:

(16) $$\hat{m} = \hat{n},$$

(17) $$\hat{m}^* = \hat{n}^*.$$

Equation (13) is a Phillips curve relating $\hat{q}$ to $\hat{n}$. It shows that, with $\hat{s} = 0$, increases in n must be accompanied by increases in p and therefore in q; with $\hat{n}$ and therefore $\hat{p}$ equal to zero, an increase in s implies an increase in q. Equation (14) shows the same relationship for the foreign country. From equation (15) we see that, if n increases, there is excess supply of goods in the home market; excess demand, instead, may derive from an increase in n* and in s. Under the assumption that monetary authorities have full information about disturbances, they can control employment deviations. Therefore, n and n* can be considered the instruments instead of m and m*.

The utility functions of the monetary authorities are:

(18) $$U = -\tfrac{1}{2}(\mu\hat{n}^2 + \hat{q}^2),$$

(19) $$U^* = -\tfrac{1}{2}(\mu\hat{n}^{*2} + \hat{q}^{*2}).$$

Each countries maximizes its utility over $\hat{n}$ ($\hat{n}^*$), given the other country's $\hat{n}^*$ ($\hat{n}$). Reminding the assumption that the countries are mirror images, the reduced form equations for the consumer price indices become:

(20) $$\hat{q} = [a + b^2(1-a)d]\hat{n} - b^2(1-a)d\hat{n}^* - x,$$

(21) $$\hat{q}^* = -b^2(1-a)d\hat{n} + [a + b^2(1-a)d]\hat{n}^* - x.$$

There is therefore a macroeconomic interdependence between the two countries: in particular, monetary policy of each of them imposes a negative constraint on the other one. In other words, it is a case of "beggar-thy-neighbour" policy. Monetary authorities can therefore play games in order to maximize their own utility, given the other country's behaviour.

In the absence of disturbances, i. e. with $x = 0$, substituting for $\hat{q}$ and $\hat{q}^*$ in equations (18) and (19) from equations (20) and (21) and setting $\hat{n} = \hat{n}^* = 0$ yields $\hat{q} = \hat{q}^* = 0$. This means that each authority can reach its bliss point. There is no policy conflict, no game to be described.

For $x < 0$, instead, Fig. 5 applies. From the utility functions one obtains indifference curves which have the forms of ellipses. *B* and *B** indicates the bliss points of the authorities, NS and NS* their reaction functions, which are derived substituting for $\hat{q}$ and $\hat{q}^*$ in equations (18) and (19) from equations (20) and (21) and maximizing with respect to $\hat{n}$ and $\hat{n}^*$ respectively. Point *N* indicates the Nash equilibrium solution: it is Pareto inferior, but there are no incentives to move away from it. The two countries set $\hat{n} = \hat{n}^* > 0$. The shaded area contains the points which are Pareto superior to N, while the Pareto efficient outcomes lie on the hyperbole *BFB**: at these points there is, however, an incentive to "cheat", since at least one player is not on its reaction function.

Point S is the Stackelberg solution: the leader (the foreign country in this example) chooses on the partner's reaction function the tangency point with its possible highest indifference curve. Utility is now higher for both players, but the leader has an incentive to move away from this point because it is not using an optimal reply.

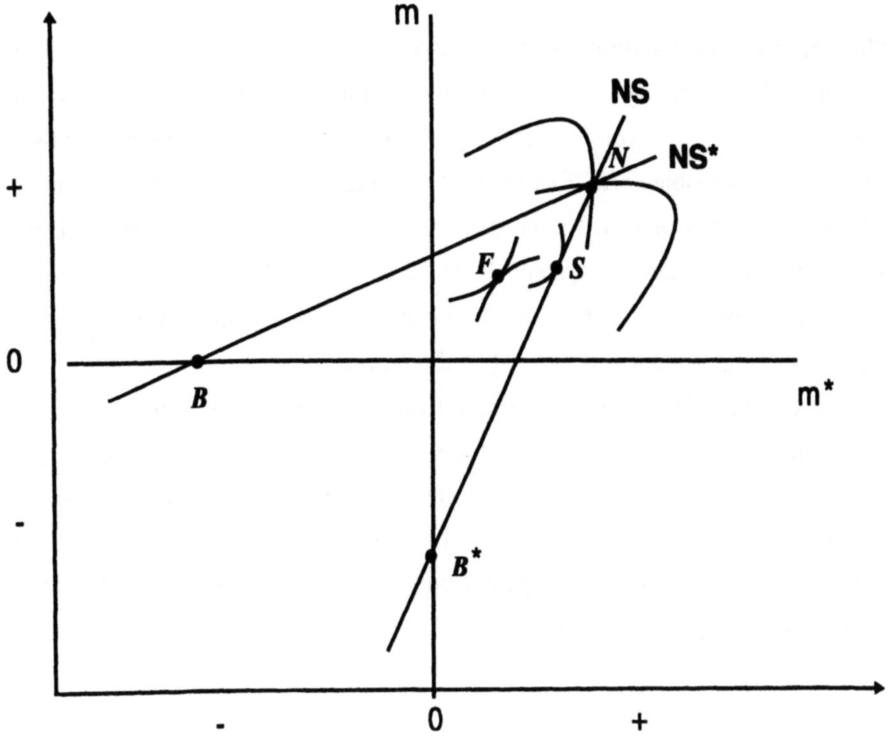

Fig. 5: The Nash, cooperative and Stackelberg solutions.

While the Nash solution corresponds to a flexible exchange rate system, the Stackelberg one is typical of a regime of transition to a monetary union, when one country, the leader, sets its monetary policy independently and the other one follows it fixing the exchange rate parity and assigning the monetary policy instrument to the exchange rate objective. The model can, however, be adapted to the case of a monetary union in which the two member-countries cooperate in maintaining the irrevocably fixed parity and varying the national money supplies in the same proportions, maximizing the sum of their utility functions.

Analytically, the problem that they face consists in maximizing the sum of equations (18) and (19) given (20), (21) and (22):

(22) $$\hat{n} = \hat{n}^*.$$

The demonstration shown by Fratianni/von Hagen does not apply to the case in which the monetary authority of one country targets price stability only. Assuming that this is true for the low inflation country, while the high inflation one also has the objective of keeping the unemployment rate low, coordination brings advantages only to the latter and it becomes difficult to find incentives for the former to join the system. It can also be noted that the model, being a two-country one, does not allow for the study of the relationship between the members of the system and the rest of the world.

The Collins (1988) model differs from the above presented one in the replacement of the shock with a predetermined portion of inflation, different for the two countries, which are completely symmetric under all other aspects. Perfect capital mobility is assumed in the model; output is demand determined and the real exchange rate expectations are static. All the variables are in logarithms, except the interest rates, and notation is as before, apart from:

i = nominal interest rate;
r = real interest rate;
y = deviation of output from full employment level;
f_t = inflation = $q_t - q_{t-1}$;
superscript e denotes expectations;
subscript t denotes time (omitted when this does not generate confusion).

The model equations are then the following:

(1a) $$y_t = as_t + by^*_t - cr_t,$$

(1b) $$y^*_t = -as_t + by_t - cr^*_t,$$

(2) $$i_t - i^*_t = e^e_{t+1} - e_t,$$

(3) $$e^e_{t+1} + p^{*e}_{t+1} - p^e_{t+1} = e_t + p^*_t - p_t,$$

(4) $$r_t = r^*_t,$$

(5a) $$p_t - p_{t-1} = f_{t-1} + gy_t,$$

(5b) $$p^*_t - p^*_{t-1} = f^*_{t-1} + gy^*_t,$$

(6a) $$q_t = lp_t + (1-l)(e_t + p^*_t) = p_t + (1-l)s_t,$$

(6b) $$q^*_t = lp^*_t + (1-l)(p_t - e_t) = p^*_t - (1-l)s_t,$$

(7a) $$m_t - p_t = y_t,$$

(7b) $$m^*_t - p^*_t = y^*_t.$$

Substituting from (5) into (7) one can see that monetary authorities can control the output level in their own country. Output can therefore be considered the instrument of monetary authorities. These want to minimize the respective loss function:

(8a) $$L = \frac{1}{2}(y^2 + \mu f^2),$$

(8b) $$L^* = \frac{1}{2}(y^{*2} + \mu f^{*2}).$$

In order to express inflation in terms of output, one must go through the following steps. Equations (1) - (4) yield:

(9) $$s = [(1+b)/2a](y - y^*),$$

(10a) $$r = -[(1-b)/2c](y + y^*),$$

(10b) $$r^* = -[(1-b)/2c](y + y^*).$$

Solving for inflation using equations (5), (6) and (9) yields:

(11a) $$f = f_0 + gy + a(y - y^*),$$

(11b) $$f^* = f^*_0 + gy^* - a(y - y^*),$$

where:

$$f_0 = f_{t-1} + (1-l)\, s_{t-1} = \text{predetermined portion of inflation;}$$

$$f^*_0 = f^*_{t-1} + (1-l)s_{t-1},$$

$$a = (1-l)(1-b)/2a.$$

Substituting into (8) and taking the first order derivatives, the first order conditions yield the following reaction functions:

(15a) $$y = v\,(ay^* - f_0),$$

(15b) $$y^* = v\,(ay - f^*_0),$$

where:

$$v = [\mu(g+a)]/[1+\mu(g+a)^2].$$

The two countries, therefore, engage in a competitive deflation (the country with a higher predetermined portion of inflation deflates more). Also in this model, if $f_0 = f^*_0 = 0$, each country can reach its bliss point by setting $y = y^* = 0$, with no scope for policy games.

Also this model has a monetary union (i. e. fixed exchange rate cooperative solution) version, which is analytically derived minimizing the sum of (8a) and (8b) subject to (11a), (11b) and (16):

(16) $$y = y^*,$$

which yields the following first order condition:

(17) $$y = -(f_0 + f^*_0)/2\mu g/(1+\mu g^2) = y^*.$$

The two models presented deal with monetary policy. De Grauwe (1990), instead, analyses the coordination of fiscal policies. The model is again a two-country one. The system of interdependence is derived from the Mundell-Fleming model, each national authority is assumed to minimize a loss function having output and the current account of the balance of payments as arguments. The conclusion is that a coordinated response to exogenous disturbances generally improves welfare, but that, in the case of the EMS countries, there is little incentive to cooperate.

The models analysed, though concerning the transition phase to a monetary union rather than stabilization policy within a single currency area, can nevertheless be interpreted also as the proposal of a new criterion for the determination of the optimal dimension of a currency area, that of the *degree of policy coordination* among the countries concerned.

Conclusions

Apart from the purpose of offering an overview of the state of the art for the single currency area literature, this chapter was also aimed to show two main points: the necessity of a connection between the macroanalysis, centred on stabilization policy, and the microeconomic interest for the optimality issue; and the sometimes neglected importance of the change in structural parameters brought about by the unification process: a geometrical demonstration of the influence of this phenomenon has also been provided with reference to the inflation-unemployment trade-off.

Bibliography

Bean, C. R. (1992): "Economic and Monetary Union in Europe", in: *Journal of Economic Perspectives*, Vol. 6, Nr. 4, p. 31-52.

Bertola, G. (1989): "Factor Flexibility, Uncertainty and Exchange Rate Regimes", in: De Cecco, M.; Giovannini, G. (eds.), *A European Central Bank?*, London.

Canzoneri, M. B.; Henderson, D. W. (1988): "Is Sovereign Policy Making Bad?", in: Brunner, K.; Meltzer, A. H. (eds.), *Stabilization Policy and Labour Markets*, Carnegie Rochester Conference Series on Public Policy, 28.

Collins, S. (1988): "Inflation and the EMS", *NBER Working Paper* Nr. 2599.

Corden, M. (1972): "Monetary Integration", in: *Essays in International Finance* Nr. 93, Princeton.

De Grauwe, Paul (1975): "Conditions for a monetary Union", *Weltwirtschaftliches Archiv*, Bd 111.

De Grauwe, Paul (1990): "Fiscal Policy in the EMS-A Strategic Analysis", in: Claassen,E.-M. (ed.), *International and European Monetary Systems*, Oxford.

Eichengreen, B. (1990): "Costs and Benefits of European Monetary Unification", *CEPR Discussion Paper* Nr. 453.

Feuerstein, S.; Siebke, J. (1990): "Wechselkursunion und Stabilitätspolitik", in: *Zeitschrift für Wirtschafts- u. Sozialwissenschaften* 110, p. 359-379.

Feuerstein, S. (1992): *Studien zur Wechselkursunion*, Heidelberg.

Fleming, M. (1971): "On Exchange Rate Unification", in: *Economic Journal*, Nr.323, Vol. 81, p. 467-488 and Essays on Economic Policy, New York, p. 233-260, 1978.

Fratianni, M.; von Hagen, J. (1990): "The European Monetary System Ten Years After", in: *Carnegie-Rochester Conference Series on Public Policy*, Vol. 32, p. 173-242.

Gandolfo, G. (1986): *Economia internazionale*, Tomo secondo, Torino, p. 470-474.

Kenen, P. B. (1969): "The Theory of Optimum Currency Areas: An Eclectic View", in: Mundell, R. A.; Swoboda, A. K. (eds.), *Monetary Problems of the International Economy, Chicago*, p. 41-60.

Levin, J. H. (1983): "A Model of Stabilization Policy in a Jointly Floating Currency Area", in: Bhandari, J. S.; Putnam, B. H. (eds.), *Economic Interdependence and Flexible Exchange Rates*, Cambridge (Mass.), London, p. 329-349.

McKinnon, R. (1963): "Optimum Currency Areas", in: *American Economic Review*, Vol. 53, p. 717-725.

Moutos, T.; Scarth, W. (1988): "Stabilization Policy within a Currency Area", in: *Scottish Journal of Political Economy* 35, p. 387-397.

Mundell, R. (1961): "A Theory of Optimum Currency Areas", in: *American Economic Review*, Vol. 51, p. 657-665.

Mussa, M. (1979): "Macroeconomic Interdependence and the Exchange Rate Regime", in: Dornbusch, R.; Frenkel, J. (eds.), *International Economic Policy*, Baltimore, London, Ch.5.

Pace, C. (1978): *Impact of Dollar Fluctuations on European Unification*, New York.

Sauernheimer, K. (1984): "Fiscal Policy in einer Wechselkursunion", in: *Finanzarchiv*, p. 143-157.

Sauernheimer, K. (1991): "Wirtschaftspolitische Interdependenz in einer Wechselkursunion", in: Siebke, J. (ed.), *Monetärische Konfliktfelder der Weltwirtschaft*, Berlin 1991, p. 113-124.

Senn, L. (1992): "The Joint Effects of the Completion of the Internal Market and European Monetary Union on Regional Economies", in: *Rivista Internazionale di Scienze Sociali*, Nr. 1, p. 173-189.

Thomsen, U. (1992): "Stabilitätspolitik in einer kleinen Wechselkursunion bei festem externen Wechselkurs", *Diskussionbeiträge aus dem Institut für Theoretische Volkswirtschaftslehre der Universität Kiel* Nr. 90.

Vaubel, R. (1978): "Strategies for Currency Unification", *Kieler Studien* Nr. 156, Tübingen.

Willms, M. (1991): "German Monetary Unification and European Monetary Union: Theoretical Issues and Strategic Policy Problems", in: Welfens, P.J.J. (Ed.), *European Monetary Integration*, Berlin, Heidelberg, New York, p. 133-157.

Willms, M. (1992): *Internationale Währungspolitik*, München.

Wohltmann, H.-W. (1993): "Transmission nationaler Wirtschaftspolitiken in einer Wechselkursunion", *Jahrbücher für Nationalökonomie und Statistik* 211, p. 73-89.

CHAPTER II

AN IS-LM-AS MODEL FOR A "SMALL" EXCHANGE RATE UNION

Introduction

The following is an analysis of stabilization policy in an exchange rate union and an attempt to link the micro- and macroeconomic aspects of the problem. The role played by the rest of the world is also considered. This is accomplished using an IS-LM-AS three-country model, in which no symmetry in the union member-countries is assumed, similar to that developed in De Bonis (1992). This allows the study of the problem of the union cohesion, with respect to the efficacy of policy and its relationships with the mobility of factors and the incidence of economic shocks.

1. The model

The complete model and simplifications introduced for computational reasons

The essential characteristics of a monetary union, in the definition used in the literature [see for all Allen (1976), Willet/Tower (1976), Padoa Schioppa (1986) and Basevi (1986)] are: (a) the adoption of a single currency for the member-countries, or the fixing of parities at which currencies are mutually convertible (in this case the term exchange rate union is used); (b) a common external exchange rate policy, since there can be only a unique exchange rate between a foreign currency and the union one; (c) the existence of a central monetary authority and the pooling of foreign exchange reserves, which ensures the aim of maintaining fixed exchange rate relationships within the union.

If fixed exchange rates between member-countries are combined with flexible exchange rates towards the rest of the world, the analysis of macroeconomic policies requires the construction of three-component models, which allow the study of the relationships between a union member-country, the rest of the union and the rest of the world. A way of accomplishing this is to modify the basic Mundell-Fleming model, which is formed by a goods market, a money market and an aggregate supply/aggregate demand equilibrium equations for one country. For simplicity it will be assumed that the union consists of only two countries.

The first step of the modification consists in adding the same equations for a second country, i.e. the other member of the union. The second step concerns the money market equilibrium equations: given the constraint imposed by the irrevocably fixed exchange rates within the union, the national central banks cannot control the money supply within their country, which is therefore endogenous, and the money market is a single one for the whole union. Consequently, there will be only one money market equilibrium equation.

There are four more qualifications to be considered:

(1) The supply of goods in the union member-countries is assumed to be dependent on the real exchange rate towards the rest of the world and the other union member-country. This corresponds to the case when workers take their decisions on the supply of labour with regard to the level of their "consumption wage". Then, an appreciation of the exchange rate makes foreign goods cheaper and increases the purchasing power of the domestic wage, thus leading to an increase in the supply of labour for a given level of the nominal wage. Therefore, the real exchange rate is a shift variable of the aggregate supply curve.

(2) The demand for money is assumed to depend on the consumer price index rather than on the price of the domestic product.

(3) Perfect capital mobility is assumed both within the union and between the union and the rest of the world.

(4) The intra-currency area exchange rate is normalized to unity.

The model is then the following:

1.1 $$Y_1 = C_1(\overset{+}{Y_1}, \overset{-}{r_w}) + G_1 + B_1(\overset{+}{P_2/P_1}, \overset{-}{Y_1}, \overset{+}{Y_2}, \overset{+}{EP_w/P_1}, \overset{+}{Y_w})$$
(IS curve for country 1)

1.2 $$Y_2 = C_2(\overset{+}{Y_2}, \overset{-}{r_w}) + G_2 + B_2(\overset{+}{P_1/P_2}, \overset{+}{Y_1}, \overset{-}{Y_2}, \overset{+}{EP_w/P_2}, \overset{+}{Y_w})$$
(IS curve for country 2)

1.3 $$M_1 + M_2 + R = Q_1L_1(\overset{+}{Y_1}, \overset{-}{r_w}) + Q_2L_2(\overset{+}{Y_2}, \overset{-}{r_w})$$
(LM curve for the union)

1.4 $$Y_1 = Y_1^s(\overset{-}{EP_w/P_1}, \overset{-}{P_2/P_1})$$
(AS-AD equilibrium equation for country 1; its aggregate supply function is: $Y_1^s = Y_1^s(EP_w/P_1, P_2/P_1)$)

1.5 $$Y_2 = Y_2^s(\overset{-}{EP_w/P_2}, \overset{-}{P_1/P_2})$$
(same as above for country 2)

where, for i = 1, 2:
B_i = country i's net exports;
C_i = private expenditure on consumption and investment goods in country i;
E_i = exchange rate towards the rest of the world;
G_i = government expenditure in country i;
L_i = money demand in country i;
M_i = central bank's holding of domestic securities in country i;
P_i = country i's price level;
Q_i = country i's consumer price index ($= a_iP_i + a_jP_j + a_wEP_w$, $a_i + a_j + a_w = 1$);
R = total international reserves held by the central banks of the union;
r_w = world interest rate;
Y_i = country i's output;
Y_w = world output;

and the signs above the arguments of the functions indicate the sign of the partial derivative.

The endogenous variables of the system are: Y_1, Y_2, P_1, P_2, E. The exogenous variables are: G_1, G_2, M_1, M_2, r_w, Y_w.

If Y_w were not considered exogenously fixed (economic changes in the currency area would then have strong repercussions on the world demand for its exports), the monetary union would be so big in an economic sense as to affect world economic variables and one could integrate the effects of the increased "weight" of the countries when forming a union through making Y_w endogenous.

The complexity of the model suggests to limit the analysis, in a first moment, to the demand side, in order to better understand the mechanisms operating there. It is then initially assumed that both P_1 and P_2 equal the exogenously fixed P_w. The later introduction of the supply-side, however, will substantially modify the results obtained in this first part of the analysis.

Moreover, the effects of policy operations will be initially shown for the case of the money demand depending on the domestic price level rather than on the consumer price index and the supply of goods only on the real exchange rate towards the rest of the world. The simplified model will then be:

1.1* $$Y_1 = C_1\,(Y_1, r_w) + G_1 + B_1\,(P_2/P_1, Y_1, Y_2, EP_w/P_1, Y_w)$$

1.2* $$Y_2 = C_2\,(Y_2, r_w) + G_2 + B_2\,(P_1/P_2, Y_1, Y_2, EP_w/P_2, Y_w)$$

1.3* $$M_1 + M_2 + R = P_1L_1\,(Y_1, r_w) + P_2L_2\,(Y_2, r_w)$$

1.4* $$Y_1 = Y_1\,(EP_w/P_1)$$

1.5* $$Y_2 = Y_2\,(EP_w/P_2).$$

The labour market and Phillips curve foundations of the AS curve used in the model

Before going to the analysis of the effects of monetary and fiscal policy, it is convenient to show the Phillips curve foundations of the type of aggregate supply curve used in the model. The Phillips curve, elaborated by Phillips (1958), represents the relationship between the rate of change of the nominal wage ($\dot{W}$) and, in a general formulation, the variable describing the situation in the labour market (L) and a vector of other relevant factors (**z**):

(1) $$\dot{W} = f(L, \mathbf{z}).$$

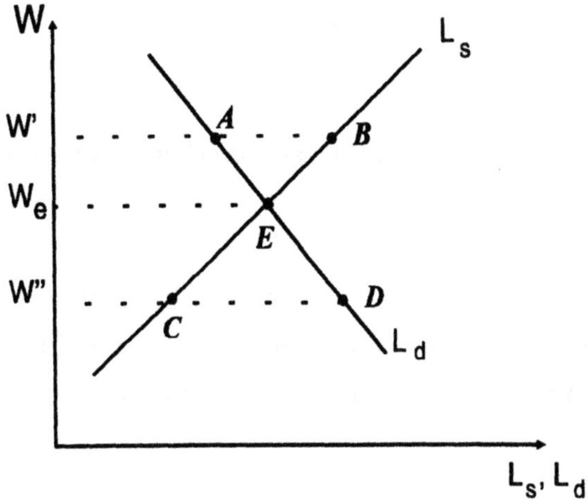

Fig. 1: The labour market equilibrium.

The starting point of the analysis is the labour market, the equilibrium of which is represented in Fig. 1, where the supply of labour is indicated by the L^S curve and the demand for labour by the L^D curve: it is shown that, when the demand for labour is high relatively to the supply of it, the wage rises, and, conversely, when the demand is low relatively to the supply, the wage falls. Phillips also pointed out that the rate of rise (fall) would be greater, the greater the excess (deficiency) of demand.

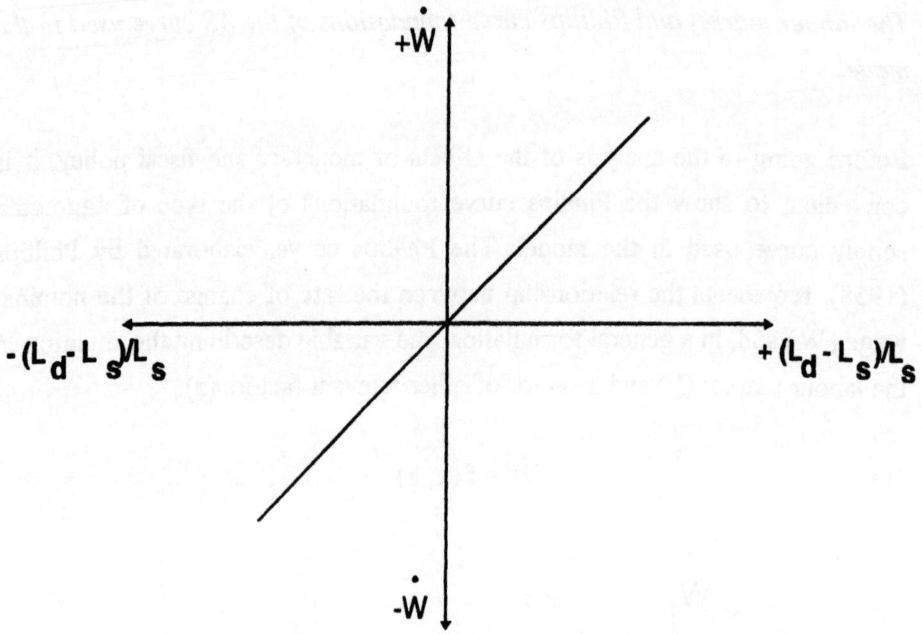

Fig.2: The relationship between excess demand of labour and wage changes.

This was given a graphical representation by Lipsey (1960), which is reproduced in Fig. 2. On this basis, one can write the following relationship between $\dot{W}$ and the ratio of excess demand over labour supply:

(2) $$\dot{W} = f\,[(L^D - L^S)/L^S].$$

Being the disequilibrium on the labour market difficult to be observed, Phillips used the quota of unemployed workers, i. e. the ratio of registered unemployed over the sum of employed and unemployed workers (u). The relationship between the disequilibrium in the labour market and the share of unemployment was represented by Lipsey as reproduced in Fig. 3, where point u* indicates the existence of frictional and seasonal unemployment, consistent with the labour market being in equilibrium.

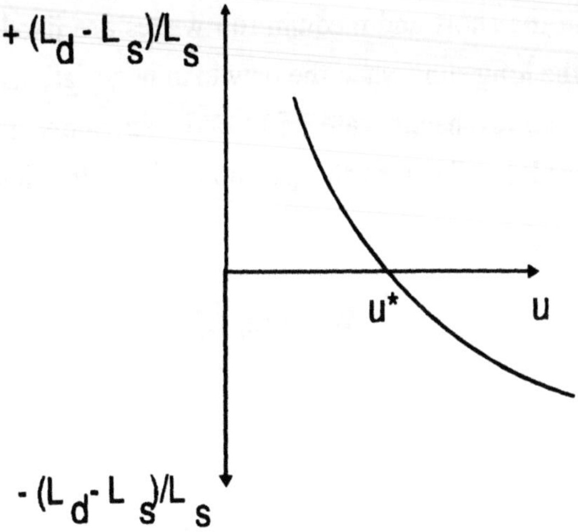

Fig. 3: The unemployment and labour market disequilibrium relationship.

The combination of Fig. 2 and Fig. 3 yields the representation of the relationship between the share of unemployment and the rate of change of the money wage rate, illustrated in Fig. 4.

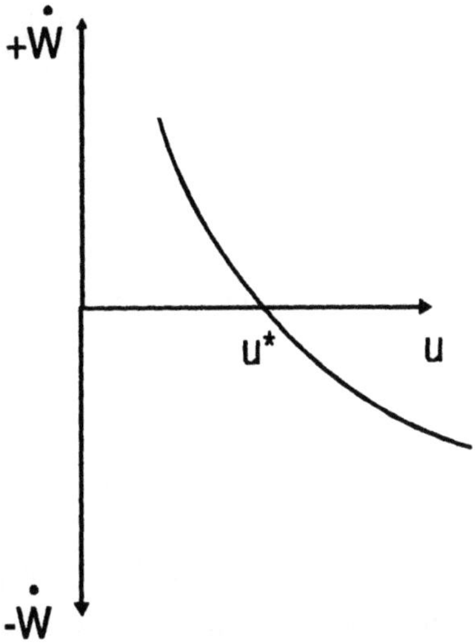

Fig. 4: The relationship between the share of unemployment and the rate of change of the money wage rate.

Supposing that in the short and medium run wages are fixed in nominal terms and that only in the long run (when the new loan negotiations take place) these are indexed to the exchange rate (E), one can show that the expected depreciation rate ($\dot{E}$) influences the position of the Phillips curve, which is now defined as:

(3) $$\dot{W} = f(u, \dot{E})$$

and represented in Fig. 5.

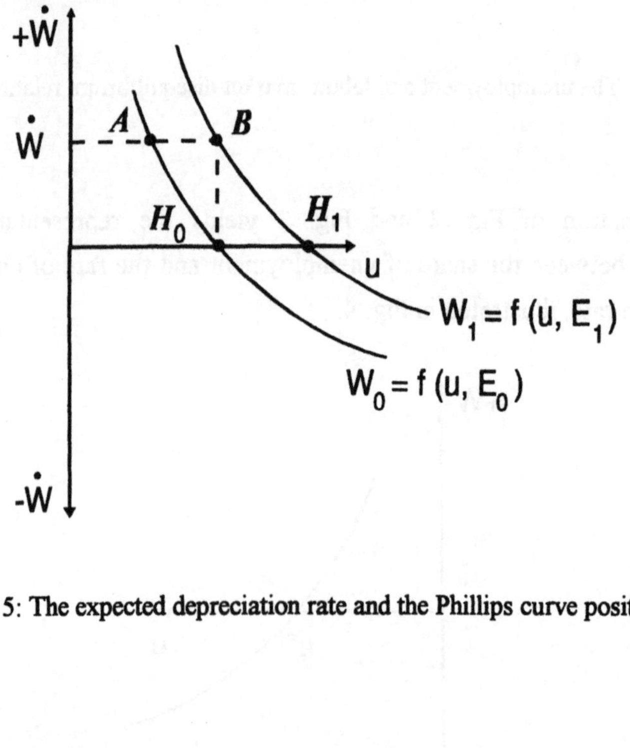

Fig. 5: The expected depreciation rate and the Phillips curve position.

Point H_0 corresponds to unemployment being equal to its frictional and seasonal components and the labour market being in equilibrium. A depreciation, causing an increase in the demand for domestic produced goods, pushes enterpreneurs to increase the demand for labour at the existing nominal wages. Labour supply being momentaneously unaffected, this increases W and reduces u, bringing the economy to point A.

In the next negotiation round, however, the attempt of the workers to preserve the purchasing power of the wage will induce an increase in the nominal wage rate proportional to the depreciation rate. This means that each unemployment rate is now connected with a higher $\dot{W}$, i. e. the Phillips curve has shifted to the right. The wage rate is now consistent with the initial unemployment rate, H_0. In terms of the aggregate supply curve, this means that in the long run it shifts according to the changes in the exchange rate. This can be shown algebraically as follows.

The "exchange rate augmented" Phillips curve can be expressed as:

$$(W - W_{-1})/W_{-1} = - \mu\ (u - u^*) + b\ (E - E_{-1})/E_{-1} \tag{4}$$

which can also be written:

$$W = W_{-1}\ [1 - \mu\ (u - u^*) + b\ (E - E_{-1})/E_{-1}]. \tag{5}$$

Expressing u as the ratio between the unemployed (U) and the total labour force (LF), one gets:

$$W = W_{-1}\ \{1 - \mu\ [(L + U - L)/LF - (L^* + U^* - L^*)/LF] + b\ (E - E_{-1})/E_{-1}\} \tag{6}$$

$$W = W_{-1}\ [1 - \mu\ (L^* - L)/LF + b\ (E - E_{-1})/E_{-1}]. \tag{7}$$

Given a simplified production function of the form:

$$Y = L, \tag{8}$$

one obtains:

$$W = W_{-1}\ [1 - \mu\ (Y - Y^*)/LF + b\ (E - E_{-1})/E_{-1}]. \tag{9}$$

With the mark-up function:

(10) $$W = P$$

and substituting, one gets:

(11) $$P = P_{-1} [1 + \mu (Y - Y^*)/LF + b (E - E_{-1})/E_{-1}],$$

where the rate of change of the exchange rate appears as a shifting parameter. Moreover, this aggregate supply curve is upward sloping even in a classical environment. This last point can be seen considering that, given a general production technology:

(12) $$Y = f(L, K),$$

the demand for labour will be:

(13) $$W/P = f_L (L^D, K),$$

while the supply of labour depends on the consumption wage:

(14) $$W/Q = h (L^S),$$

Q, the consumer price index, being equal to $P^t(EP^*)^{1-t}$, where P^* is the price of foreign product and t the share of imports.

If the domestic price level changes by 5% and so does the nominal wage, the real wage will be unchanged and the labour demand curve shifts upwards proportionally in the (L, W) space. Since the price of imported goods has not risen, the consumer price index rises by less than 5% (the labour supply schedule shifts upwards less than the labour demand one). Therefore, one has a locus of equilibria which gives an upward sloping aggregate supply curve in the (y, P) space, as illustrated in Fig. 6.

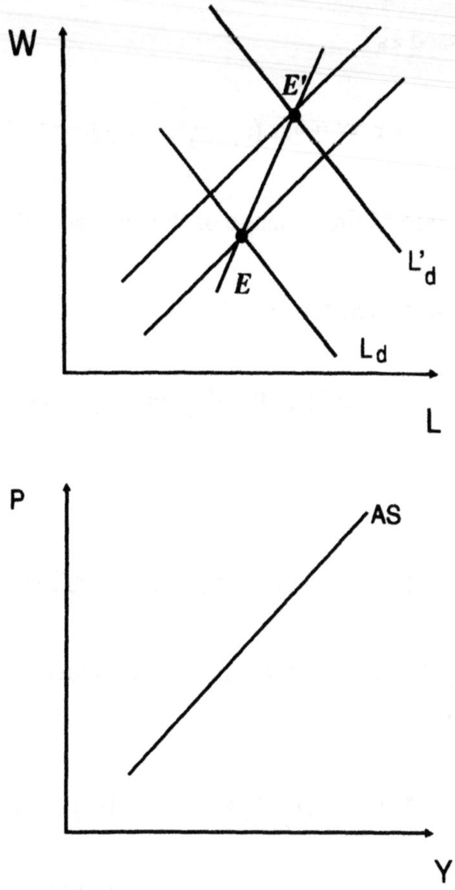

Fig. 6: The upward sloping aggregate supply curve.

This analysis provides a Phillips curve foundation of the simplified aggregate supply curve $Y_i = Y_i\ (EP_w/P_i)$. The augmenting term is, therefore, the rate of change of the expected nominal exchange rate towards the rest of the world, on the assumption of P_w being exogenously fixed. A more general treatment must consider, instead, the rate of change of the consumer price index, $\dot{Q}_i$, where $\dot{Q}_i=(P_j)^a(EP_w)^b(P_i)^{(1-a-b)}$, where subscripts i, j denote member countries' economic variables, subscript w rest of the world ones, and a, b the share of imported goods (from countries j and w to country i). The Phillips curve is then defined as:

(15) $$\dot{W}_i = f\,(u_i, \dot{Q})$$

which can be expressed as :

(16) $$r_w W = - \mu (u_i - u_i^*) + r_Q Q_i$$

where r denotes the rate of time change of the corresponding variable.

Equation (16) can also be written as:

(17) $$r_w W_i = - \mu(u_i-u_i^*)[br_j P_j+a(r_E E+r_w P_w)+(1-a-b)r_j P_j]$$

and, given (10):

(18) $$r_i P_i = [1/(a+b)]\{-\mu(u_i-u_i^*)+[br_j P_j+a(r_E E+r_w P_w)]\}.$$

Defining u as in page 57, given equation (8) and following the same procedure as above, one obtains:

(19) $$P_i = P_{i-1}\{1-\mu(Y-Y^*)/LF+[b(P_j-P_{j-1})/P_{j-1}+a(E-E_{-1})/E_{-1}+a(P_w-P_{w-1})/P_{w-1}]\}.$$

The rate of change in P_2, E and P_w are now all shift parameters of the AS curve. For a different derivation of this result see Feuerstein (1992).

2. The efficacy of monetary policy

The short run

The introduction of the assumption that country 1's price level is equal to country 2's and both are equal to the world one, normalized to unity, allows the following simplification of the model, which draws on Levin (1983):

2.1 $$Y_1 = C_1 (Y_1, r_w) + G_1 + B_1 (Y_1, Y_2, Y_w, E)$$

2.2 $$Y_2 = C_2 (Y_2, r_w) + G_2 + B_2 (Y_1, Y_2, Y_w, E)$$

2.3 $M_1 + M_2 + R = L_1 (Y_1, r_w) + L_2 (Y_2, r_w)$

The endogenous variables of the system become three: Y_1, Y_2, E.

The effects of an increase in country 1's money stock will now be considered. A particular attention will be given to the influence of the relative size of the union member-countries on the results. It is possible to study the effects of stabilization policies through a graphical analysis, adapting the two-country Keynesian model. The EE-schedule in Fig. 7 shows the combinations of Y_1 and Y_2 consistent with the goods market equilibrium in the currency area and is derived varying parametrically the exchange rate between the union and the rest of the world.

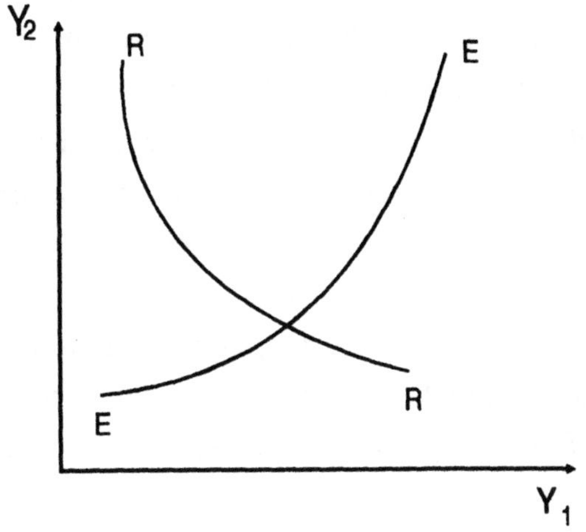

Fig. 7: Equilibrium in the extended two-country Keynesian model.

The schedule is *upward* sloping, since an increase in E improves the union member-countries trade balance, thus increasing Y_1 and Y_2 (the elasticity conditions are assumed to hold); a further increase is induced by the trade linkage effect operating between country 1 and country 2. This can be shown differentiating 2.1 and 2.2 w.r.t. E:

$$dY_1/dE = [B_{1E} (1-C_{2Y2}-B_{2Y2}) + B_{2E} B_{1Y2}]/|D| > 0,$$

where $|D|$ equals $(1\text{-}C_{1Y1}\text{-}B_{1Y1})\,(1\text{-}C_{2Y2}\text{-}B_{2Y2}) - B_{2Y1}B_{1Y2}$.

Dividing through by $(1\text{-}C_{2Y2}\text{-}B_{2Y2})$, the numerator becomes B_{1E} (which shows the direct aggregate demand effect) $+ B_{2E}B_{1Y2}/(1\text{-}C_{2Y2}\text{-}B_{2Y2})$ (the trade linkage effect for country 1). The same applies to country 2:

$$dY_2/dE = [B_{2E}\,(1\text{-}C_{1Y1}\text{-}B_{1Y1})\,B_{2E} + B_{1E}\,B_{2Y1}]/|D| > 0.$$

Thus, dividing dY_2/dE by dY_1/dE, one obtains the slope of the EE schedule:

$$dY_2/dY_1 = [B_{1E}\,(1\text{-}C_{2Y2}\text{-}B_{2Y2}) + B_{2E}B_{1Y2}]/[B_{2E}\,(1\text{-}C_{1Y1}\text{-}B_{1Y1}) + B_{1E}B_{2Y1}] > 0.$$

It can be noted that the EE curve is downward sloping in the two-country Keynesian model, where the schedule is derived through varying parametrically the exchange rate between country 1 and country 2.

The RR-schedule shows the combinations of Y_1 and Y_2 consistent with equilibrium in the financial sector, given that, with perfect capital mobility, the interest rate in country 1 must equal that of country 2 and the world one. The curve is upward sloping in the two-country case, but *downward* sloping in this set up: if Y_1 increases, L_1 increases, too, exerting an upward pressure on the currency area rate of interest. To keep it down at the world level, a reduction in Y_2 and therefore in L_2 becomes necessary. Algebraically, this can be expressed in terms of the characteristics of the demand for money by differentiating eqn. 2.3:

$$dY_2/dY_1 = - L_{1Y1}/L_{2Y2}.$$

Points below and on the left of the RR-schedule correspond to a situation of excess supply of money. The opposite is true for points above and on the right of it.

Let us now examine the effects of an increase in country 1's domestic credit (see Fig. 8). An increase in M_1 requires a higher Y_1 for any given level of Y_2 to keep the money market in equilibrium. This means that the RR-schedule has shifted to the right because of this operation.

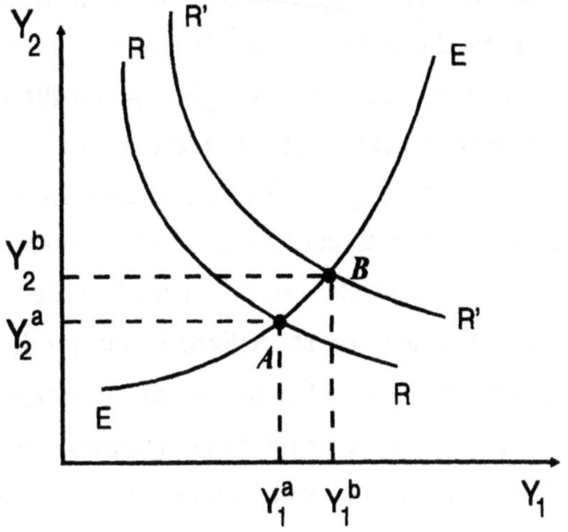

Fig. 8: The effects of an expansionary monetary policy operation.

At the initial level of income, Y_1^a and Y_2^a, the supply of money exceeds the demand for money: the downward pressure on the currency area rate of interest causes a capital outflow. The exchange rate thus depreciates to guarantee the financial sector equilibrium. The depreciation causes an increase in Y_1 and Y_2 through the balance of trade effect. The mathematics of the system yield:

$$dY_1/dM_1 = [B_{1E}\,(1\text{-}C_{2Y2}\text{-}B_{2Y2}) + B_{1Y2}\,B_{2E}]/|D_s| > 0;$$

$$dY_2/dM_1 = [B_{2E}\,(1\text{-}C_{1Y1}\text{-}B_{1Y1}) + B_{2Y1}\,B_{1E}]/|D_s| > 0;$$

$$dE/dM_1 = [(1\text{-}C_{1Y1}\text{-}B_{1Y1})(1\text{-}C_{2Y2}\text{-}B_{2Y2}) + B_{1Y2}B_{2Y1}]/|D_s| > 0;$$

where:

$$|D_s| = B_{1E}[B_{2Y1}L_{2Y2}+(1\text{-}C_{2Y2}\text{-}B_{2Y2})L_{1Y1}]+B_{2E}[B_{1Y21}L_{1Y1}+(1\text{-}C_{1Y1}\text{-}B_{1Y1})L_{2Y2}].$$

It can be noted that the expansionary effect of monetary policy works through the responsiveness of the trade balance to the depreciation of the exchange rate towards the rest of the world, B_{iE}, and does not depend on which country undertakes the operation. The ratio between the induced increases in Y_1 and Y_2 directly depends on the ratio between B_{1E} and B_{2E}: for instance, as B_{1E} increases, the expansion in country 1 is higher, given the depreciation of E; therefore, the increase in the exchange rate required for the equilibrium in the financial sector is smaller and, given B_{2E}, the expansion in country 2 is also smaller. The size of B_{iE} depends, among other factors, on how import-oriented consumption in country i is, which in turn is related to the size of the country: if this is small, it will probably be specialized in the production of a limited number of goods; therefore, a lot of goods in the consumption basket will be imported ones. In addition, the substitution with domestically produced goods may be difficult. The trade balance will then be very responsive to changes in the exchange rate.

Between the two union member-countries, therefore, the one which is more open to foreign trade (i. e. with the rest of the world) and imports goods with a low degree of substitution is affected to a greater extent by monetary policy. In the case of identical responsiveness of the trade balances to changes in the exchange rate ($B_{1E} = B_{2E}$), monetary policy has the same effects in both countries, given also that all the other parameters measuring the reactions of the two countries to changes in the relevant variables are equal.

The effectiveness of monetary policy depends on the countries' relative size also for the following reason: if the monetary operation is performed by the "big" country, it will have a noticeable effect on the monetary base of the entire area and therefore on the level of activity of both countries. The converse is true when the "small" member-country is the one which undertakes the monetary policy operation. The small country is the one which bears the relatively larger effect of the adjustment process, in terms of induced changes in the level of income.

Let us now consider the case of the demand for money depending on the consumer price index, as in equation 1.3:

1.3 $$M_1 + M_2 + R = Q_1 L_1 (Y_1, r_w) + Q_2 L_2 (Y_2, r_w),$$

where:

$$Q_1 = a_1\, P_1 + a_2\, P_2 + a_w\, E\, P_w, \qquad a_1 + a_2 + a_w = 1,$$

$$Q_2 = b_1\, P_1 + b_2\, P_2 + b_w\, E\, P_w, \qquad b_1 + b_2 + b_3 = 1.$$

Since it is assumed that in the short run $P_1 = P_2 = P_w = 1$, the model becomes:

2.1 $$Y_1 = C_1\,(Y_1, r_w) + G_1 + B_1\,(Y_1, Y_2, Y_w, E)$$

2.2 $$Y_2 = C_2\,(Y_2, r_w) + G_2 + B_2\,(Y_1, Y_2, Y_w, E)$$

2.3' $$M_1 + M_2 + R = (a_1 + a_2 + a_w E) L_1(Y_1, r_w) + (b_1 + b_2 + b_w E) L_2(Y_2, r_w).$$

The multipliers obtained are:

$$dY_1/dM_1 = [B_{1Y2}\, B_{2E} + B_{1E}\,(1 - C_{2Y2} - B_{2Y2})]/|D_s'|;$$

$$dY_2/dM_1 = [B_{2Y1}\, B_{1E} + B_{2E}\,(1 - C_{1Y1} - B_{1Y1})]/|D_s'|;$$

$$dE/dM_1 = [(1 - C_{1Y1} - B_{1Y1})\,(1 - C_{2Y2} - B_{2Y2}) - B_{1Y2}\, B_{2Y1}]\,/|D_s'|,$$

where $|D_s'| = (1 - C_{1Y1} - B_{1Y1})[(1 - C_{2Y2} - B_{2Y2})(a_w L_1 + b_w L_2) + B_{2E}(b_1 + b_2 + b_w E) L_{2Y2}] + B_{2Y1}\,[-B_{1Y2}(a_w\, L_1 + b_w L_2) + B_{1E}(b_1 + b_2 + b_w E) L_{2Y2}] + (a_1 + a_2 + a_w E) L_{1Y1}\,[B_{1Y2} B_{2E} + B_{1E}(1 - C_{2Y2} - B_{2Y2})]$.

The difference with the original case is that now all the multipliers are smaller, since the denominator is larger, while the numerator is unchanged. The explanation is that the increase in the exchange rate raises the demand for nominal balances, thus exerting an upward pressure on the interest rate, with the consequence of a smaller final expansion. The dependence of the demand for money on the consumer price index, therefore, introduces real balance effects also in the short run, even if the price levels are assumed to be fixed.

The medium run

The effects of an expansionary monetary policy in one of the two union member-countries will be now analysed introducing supply-side reactions. In the medium term, prices cannot be considered fixed: equations 2.1 - 2.3 must then be replaced by 1.1* - 1.3*. However, wages do not have time to adjust to the change in prices and equations 1.4 and 1.5, which refer to a long-run context, must be replaced respectively by:

1.4' $$Y_1 = Y_1 (P_1)$$

1.5' $$Y_2 = Y_2 (P_2).$$

The initial impact of an increase in the money supply in country 1 is as described before: the decrease in the rate of interest in country 1 brings about an expansionary pressure on the demand for goods with consequent higher price and output levels. This induces an increase also in the demands for goods imported from the other union member-country. Through the trade linkage effect, therefore, the expansionary pressure is partially shifted to the other country. The first country finds itself in a situation of trade deficit; to keep the intra-union exchange rate at the fixed level, money flows out of country 1 towards country 2, with the interest rate thus increasing in the former and decreasing in the latter.

If one additionally considers the security market, there is another and more direct mechanism through which an increase in M_1 causes a decline in the rate of interest also in country 2. If the increase in the money supply is brought about through the purchase of securities held by the private sector and also residents of the other member country hold this type of securities, the decrease in the rate of interest will take place in both countries. The expansionary pressure will be the more widespread within the union, the bigger is the market domain (and the integration with other security markets) of the purchased securities.

Through the integration of the goods and security markets, therefore, the interest rate of the union tends to decline. With perfect capital mobility with the rest of the world, this causes a capital outflow, thus inducing a depreciation of the exchange rate and an improvement in competitiveness. The qualitative results obtained are the same as before: monetary policy is effective in the medium run. However, magnitudes differ: the rise of the price level consequent to the demand increase partially counteracts the expansionary effect of the policy operation.

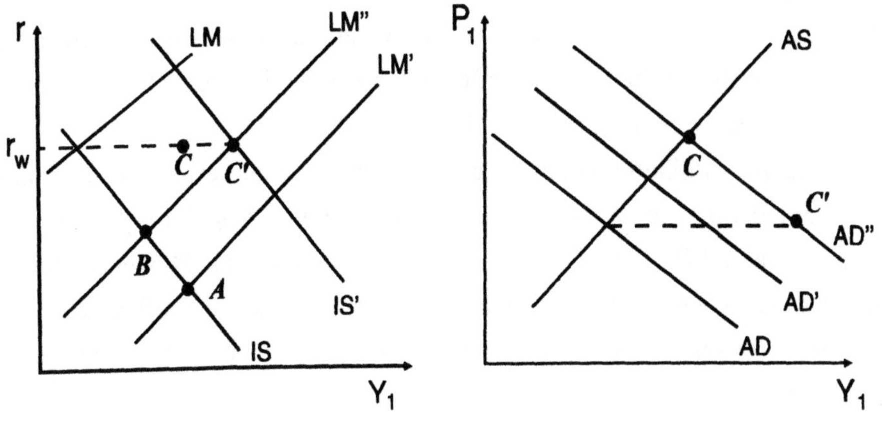

Fig. 9: The medium-run effects of an expansionary monetary policy in country 1.

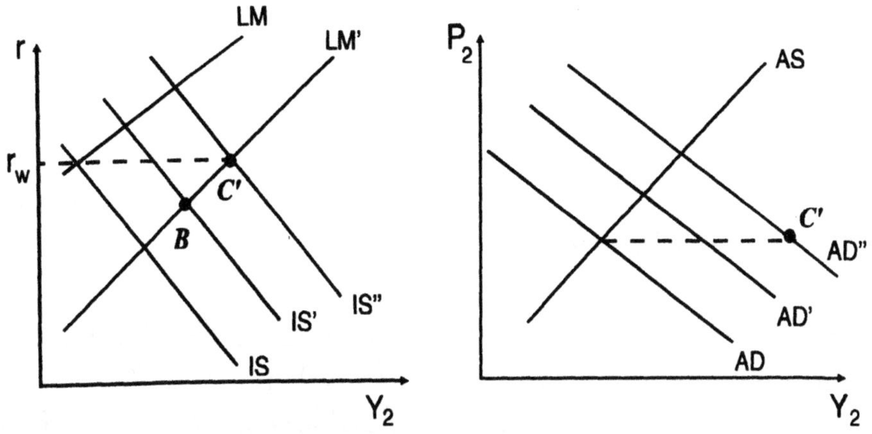

Fig. 10: The medium-run effects of an expansionary monetary policy on country 2.

This can be seen graphically (Fig. 9 for country 1 and Fig. 10 for country 2): the increase in M_1 shifts the LM curve of country 1 rightwards to LM'. At the intersection point between LM' and IS, the interest rate of country 1 would be below r_w. In a two-country model with fixed exchange rates (with the other union member-country), this would cause an instantaneous capital outflow from country 1 towards country 2. However, either through the above mentioned financial market integration and/or trade linkage mechanisms, the decrease in the interest rate will affect both union member-countries: the LM curve of country 2 will also shift to LM' (while its IS curve might shift to the right because of the trade surplus with country 1 and conversely the LM' curve of country 1 to the left because of the deficit; the results of the precedent section have shown that the final effect on the union interest rate is negative). The AD curves of both countries shift to the right.

At the new equilibrium points, marked with *B*, the interest rate of the union is below the world level. This causes a depreciation of E and a rightward shift of the IS (and AD) curves of the union member-countries. However, the AS curves of the member countries are not supposed to have an infinite elasticity as in the previous section. The increase in output will then be limited by the price rise and the final expansionary effect, denoted by point *C*, will be smaller than that in the short run, corresponding to point *C'* (the IS and LM curves of the union member-countries are shifted back by the price increase).

The results are also shown by the multipliers:

$$dY_1/dM_1 = \{B_{1s}[(1-C_{2Y2}-B_{2Y2})(Y^s_{1P1}Y^s_{2P2})+B_{2P1/P2}P_1Y^s_{1P1}/P_2^2]-B_{2s}[-B_{1Y2}(Y^s_{1P1}Y^s_{2P2})-Y^s_{1P1}B_{1P2/P1}/P_1]\}/|D_m| > 0;$$

$$dY_2/dM_1 = \{-B_{2s}[(1-C_{1Y1}-B_{1Y1})(Y^s_{1P1}Y^s_{2P2})+B_{1P2/P1}P_2Y^s_{2P2}/P_1^2]+B_{1s}[-B_{2Y1}(Y^s_{1P1}Y^s_{2P2})-Y^s_{2P2}B_{2P1/P2}/P_2]\}/|D_m| > 0;$$

where $|D_m|$ equals $-B_{1s}\{-B_{2Y1}[P_2L_{2Y2}Y^s_{1P1}Y^s_{2P2}+Y^s_{1P1}L_2]-P_1L_{1Y1}[Y^s_{1P1}Y^s_{2P2}+Y^s_{1P1}B_{2P1/P2}P_1/P_2^2]+B_{2P1/P2}/P_2-P_2L_{2Y2}Y^s_{2P2}-L_2]+L_1[Y^s_{2P2}(1-C_{2Y2}-B_{2Y2})-B_{2P1/P2}P_1/P_2^2]\}-B_{2s}\{(1-C_{1Y1}B_{1Y1})[P_2L_{2Y2}Y^s_{1P1}Y^s_{2Y2}+Y^s_{1P1}L_2] - P_1L_{1Y1}[B_{1Y2}\ Y^s_{1P1}\ Y^s_{2P2}\ Y^s_{1P1}B_{1P2/P1}/P_1]-B_{1P2/P1}P_2/P_1^2[-P_2L_{2Y2}Y^s_{2P2}-L_2]-L_1[B_{1Y2}Y^s_{2P2}+B_{1P2/P1}/P_1]\}$

and s is the real exchange rate with the rest of the world.

The multipliers are still positive, but smaller than in the short-run case, because of the positive value of the slopes of the aggregate supply curves appearing in them. In the case of the demand for money depending on the consumer price index rather than on the domestic price level, the same considerations as for the short-run case apply: the multipliers are not reported here for the sake of brevity, since they do not add much to the significance of the analysis.

The long run

The effects of monetary policy will now be considered within the framework of the complete model of equations 1.1* - 1.5*. A second effect of the exchange rate depreciation is now to be taken into account: foreign goods become more expensive for the union's consumers. Given the assumption that the supply of goods depends on the real exchange rate with the rest of the world, the aggregate supply schedules of the union member-countries shift leftwards. The consequent increase in P_1 and P_2 counteracts the initial expansion.

This can be seen graphically in Fig. 11 for country 1 and Fig. 12 for country 2.

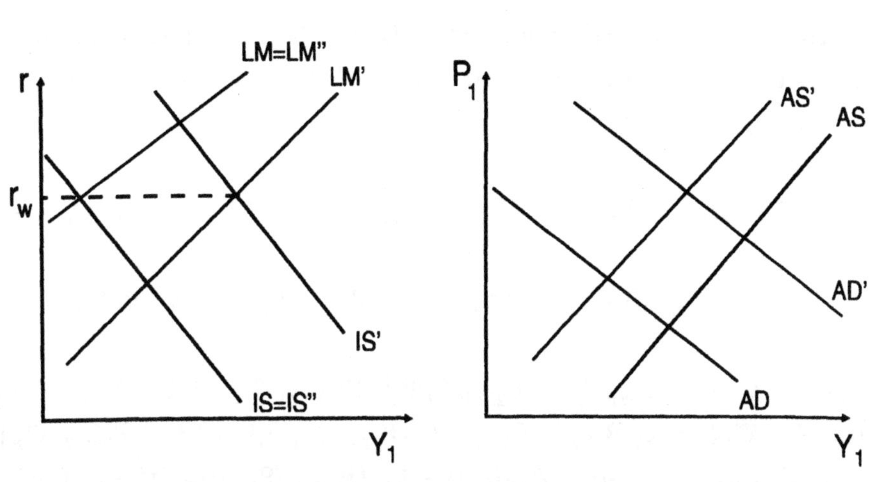

Fig. 11: The long-run ineffectiveness of an expansionary monetary policy 1.

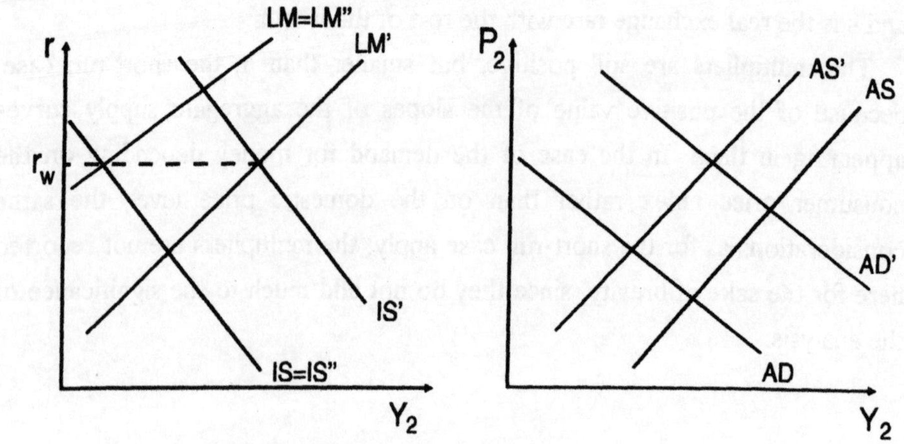

Fig. 12: The long-run ineffectiveness of an expansionary monetary policy.

The increase in M_1 shifts the LM curve of country 1 rightwards to LM'. At the intersection point between IS and LM', the interest rate would be below r_w; consequently E depreciates and IS shifts to IS'. In the (Y, P) diagram, AD shifts to AD'. However, the depreciation of E also causes a leftward shift of AS and the consequent increase in the price level makes IS' and LM' shift back. As for country 2, IS shifts to IS' because of the trade linkage mechanism and LM to LM' because of the money inflow from country 1, as above described. The other changes are the same as in country 1.

The graphical analysis cannot tell whether the final effect is positive or negative. The mathematical results derived from the system show that monetary policy is ineffective:

$$dY_1/dM_1 = [(B_{1P2/P1}B_{2P1/P2}P_1P_2Y^s_{1s} - B_{1P2/P1}B_{2P1/P2}P_1P_2Y^s_{1s})/P_{12}/P^1_2]/|D_l| \quad = 0$$

$$dY_2/dM_1 = [(B_{1P2/P1}B_{2P1/P2}P_1P_2Y^s_{1s} - B_{1P2/P1}\ B_{2P1/P2}\ P_1\ P_2Y^s_{1s})/P_{12}/P^1_2]/|D_l| = 0.$$

where $|D_l| = -B_{1P2/P1}/P_1^2\ \{-B_{2P1/P2}P_1/P_2^2\ [P_1L_{1Y1}Y^s_{1s} + P_2L_{2Y2}Y^s_{2s}] + L_2[-B_{2Y1}Y^s_{1s} - Y^s_{2s}(1-C_{2Y2}-B_{2Y2})]\} - B_{2P1/P2}/P_2\ \{B_{1P2/P1}/P_1[P_1L_{1Y1}Y^s_{1s} + P_2L_{2Y2}Y^s_{2s}] + L_2[(1-C_{1Y1}-B_{1Y1})Y^s_{1s} - B_{1Y2}Y^s_{2s} - B_{1s}]\} - L_1\ \{B_{1P2/P1}/P_1\ [-B_{2Y1}Y^s_{1s} - Y^s_{2s}(1-C_{2Y2}-B_{2Y2}) - B_{2s} + B_{2P1/P2}P_1/P_2^2\ [(1-C_{1Y1}B_{1Y1})\ Y^s_{1s} - B_{1Y2}Y^s_{2s} - B_{1s}]\}$

and s is the real exchange rate with the rest of the world.

The level of income does not change in either union member-country. The result depends on two mechanisms: the flexibility of the exchange rate towards the rest of the world and the supply-side reaction to changes in the real exchange rate. The adjustment process is therefore different from the one operating in the two-country fixed exchange rate model, though leading to the same results, and resembles instead the flexible exchange rate and price flexibility case, because of the introduction of the rest of the world as a third component.

Without supply adjustments, in fact, monetary policy would lead to an expansion in the income levels of both countries as analysed above. This differs from the result obtained using two-country models and is determined by the flexibility of the exchange rate towards the rest of the world and the corresponding balance of trade effects. These results are found also in the already existing literature on macroeconomic policy transmission in a small exchange rate union, for the exposition of which chapter 1 section 4 should be referred to.

If one applies the full model, i. e. eqns. 1.1 - 1.5, with the dependence of money demand on the consumer price index and that of aggregate supply on the real exchange rate with the other union member-country, the same results are obtained (the multipliers are not reported here since they are tediously long and complex). The effect of the introduction of the consumer price index in the demand for money are as above analysed. As for the influence of the real exchange rate with the other union member-country, being the nominal intra-union exchange rate irrevocably fixed, upward or downward pressure on the real one will result in a change of the ratio between the two domestic output price levels, i. e. P_2/P_1 for country 1 and P_1/P_2 for country 2. For instance, if the currency of country 1 tends to depreciate, e. g. because the interest rate tends to be higher than in country 2 in some phase of the adjustment process or because country 1 is in balance of payments deficit, a money outflow from country 1 to country 2 would become necessary, thus causing an increase in P_2/P_1. This would make country 2's goods more expensive for the consumers in country 1 and they would therefore reduce their supply of labour. The opposite would happen in country 2. These effects do not change, however, the long-run inefficacy result obtained for monetary policy operations.

3. The efficacy of fiscal policy

The short run

The model described by equations 2.1 - 2.3 is also useful in accounting for changes in the union member countries income levels induced by a fiscal expansion in country 1. At a given level of Y_2, Y_1 increases because of the increase in G_1. Therefore, the EE curve will shift to the right, as shown in Fig. 13.

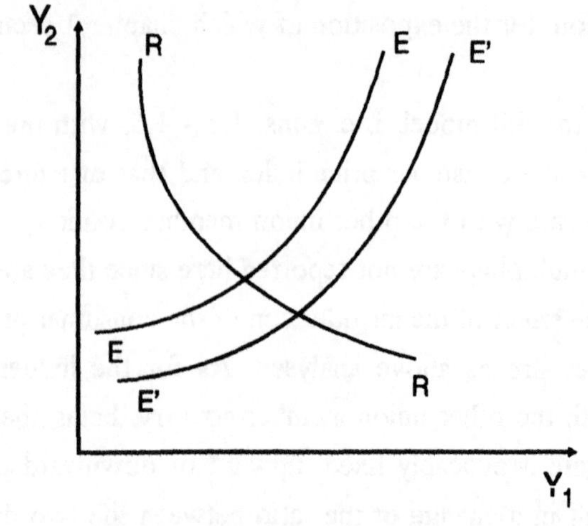

Fig. 13: The intra-union negative transmission of a fiscal expansion.

The corresponding multipliers would be:

$$dY_1/dG_1 = (B_{2E}\ L_{2Y2})/|D_s| > 0$$

$$dY_2/dG_1 = -(B_{2E}\ L_{1Y1})/|D_s| < 0$$

$$dE/dG_1 = -[B_{2Y1} L_{2Y2} + (1-C_{2Y2}-B_{2Y2}) L_{1Y1}]/|D_s| < 0.$$

The increase in G_1 induces an increase in Y_1 which in turn implies an increase in Y_2 through the trade linkage mechanism. However, given the union money supply, the higher levels of income imply an excess demand for money with respect to the original equilibrium.

The upward pressure on the rate of interest and the capital inflow can be offset by an appreciation of the exchange rate towards the rest of the world. Y_1 and Y_2 will therefore decline because of the loss in competitiveness, and the final effect on Y_2 will be contractionary.

The overall effect on the union income level, (Y_1+Y_2), will depend on the relative sensitivities of money demand in the two union member-countries. If $L_{2Y2} > L_{1Y1}$, total income will expand, and viceversa. This is because $(dY_1/dG_1)/(dY_2/dG_1)$ must equal L_{2Y2}/L_{1Y1}; given the monetary base and r_w, money demand within the union must remain at the same level as before the fiscal expansion and therefore the increase in country 1, $L_{1Y1}(dY_1/dG_1)$, must equal the contraction in country 2, $L_{2Y2}(dY_2/dG_1)$.

The short-run effectiveness of fiscal policy should then be evaluated with reference to the authorities' objective. If this is to increase the union level of income, an expansionary fiscal policy is not the appropriate instrument when it is applied in the country with a higher sensitivity of money demand to income changes. However, if the fiscal expansion in country 1 also causes an increase in Y_w, again through the trade linkage mechanism, there would also be an increase in r_w. This would reduce, if not eliminate, the need for an appreciation of the union exchange rate. Therefore, also Y_2 could eventually expand as a result of an increase in G.

Let us now consider the case of the demand for money depending on the consumer price index, as in equation 1.3:

1.3 $$M_1 + M_2 + R = Q_1 L_1 (Y_1, r_w) + Q_2 L_2 (Y_2, r_w),$$

where:

$$Q_1 = a_1 P_1 + a_2 P_2 + a_w E P_w, \qquad a_1 + a_2 + a_w = 1,$$

$$Q_2 = b_1 P_1 + b_2 P_2 + b_w E P_w, b_1 + b_2 + b_3 = 1.$$

Since it is assumed that in the short run $P_1 = P_2 = P_w = 1$, the model becomes:

$$2.1 \qquad Y_1 = C_1 (Y_1, r_w) + G_1 + B_1 (Y_1, Y_2, Y_w, E)$$

$$2.2 \qquad Y_2 = C_2 (Y_2, r_w) + G_2 + B_2 (Y_1, Y_2, Y_w, E)$$

$$2.3' \qquad M_1+M_2+R = (a_1+a_2+a_wE)L_1(Y_1,r_w)+ (b_1+b_2+b_wE) L_2(Y_2,r_w).$$

The multipliers obtained are:

$$dY_1/dG_1 = [(1-C_{2Y2}-B_{2Y2})(a_wL_1+B_wL_2)+B_{2E}(b_1+b_2+b_3E)L_{2Y2}] /|D_s'| > 0;$$

$$dY_2/dG_1 = [B_{2Y1}(a_wL_1+b_wL_2)-B_{2E}(a_1+a_2+a_wE)L_{1Y1}]/|D_s'| \gtrless 0;$$

$$dE/dG_1 = [-B_{2Y1}(b_1+b_2+b_3E)L_{2Y2}-(1-C_{2Y2}-B_{2Y2})(a_1+a_2+a_wE) L_{1Y1}]/|D_s'| < 0.$$

The major difference concerns the effect of the increase in government expenditure undertaken by country 1 on country 2's income level, the sign of which is now indeterminate, as it is in the traditional two-country model with fixed exchange rates. In fact, on the one hand, the increase in country 1's income due to the fiscal expansion exerts an upward pressure on the interest rate via the demand for money and the appreciation of E worsens the trade balance in country 2: both these effects tend to reduce Y_2. On the other hand, the appreciation of E decreases the demand for nominal money balances and the increase in Y_1 improves the trade balance in country 2: both these effects tend to increase Y_2.

Depending on which forces prevail, therefore, the level of income in one of the union member-countries can increase or decrease in response to a fiscal expansion in the other one.

The short run: differences between a tax and a bond-financed increase in government expenditure

The introduction of disposable income in the consumption and money demand functions allows the study of the effects of a balanced budget tax financed increase in government expenditure and its comparison with the bond financed case. This analysis was performed in Frenkel/Razin (1987) for the traditional Mundell-Fleming model.

The equations of the model become:

2.1° $$Y_1 = C_1 (Y_1 - T_1, r_w) + G_1 + B_1 (Y_1, Y_2, Y_w, E)$$

2.2° $$Y_2 = C_2 (Y_2 - T_2, r_w) + G_2 + B_1 (Y_1, Y_2, Y_w, E)$$

2.3° $$M_1 + M_2 + R = L_1 (Y_1 - T_1, r_w) + L_2 (Y_2 - T_2, r_w)$$

where T_i indicates direct exogenous taxes in country i.

The previous analysis still applies for a bond financed increase in government expenditure (a more rigorous treatment should involve the introduction of a wealth argument in the consumption and money demand functions).

In the case of a tax financed increase in G_1, with $dG_1 = dT_1$, we would still have a rightward shift of the EE curve, but now also the RR curve would shift: if T_1 increases, disposable income decreases and so does the demand for money; this requires a higher Y_1 to keep the money market in equilibrium, therefore the RR curve shifts to the right. This is shown in Fig. 14.

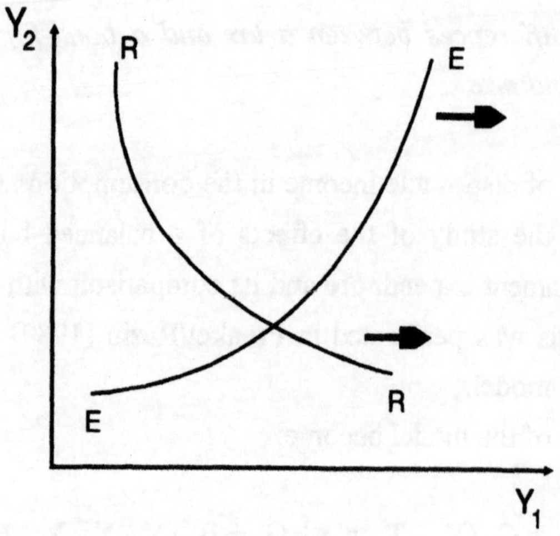

Fig. 14: Fiscal expansion with tax financing in country 1.

The corresponding multipliers are:

$dY_1/dG_1=\{B_{1E}[L_{1Y1}(1-C_{2Y2}-B_{2Y2})]+B_{2E}[L_{2Y2}(1-C_{1Y1})-L(1-C_{1Y1}+L_{1Y1}B_{1Y2}]\}/|D_s| \;\; > 0;$

$$dY_2/dG_1 = [L_{1Y1}\,(B_{1E}B_{2Y1}-B_{2E}B_{1Y1})]/|D_s| \gtrless 0;$$

$dE/dG_1 \quad = \quad \{(1-C_{1Y1})[B_{2Y1}L_{2Y2}+(1-C_{2Y2}-B_{2Y2})L_{1Y1}]+L_{1Y1}[(1-C_{1Y1}-B_{1Y1})(1-C_{2Y2}B_{2Y2})-B_{1Y2}B_{2Y1}]\}/|D_s| \gtrless 0.$

The policy effects on Y_2 and E are now uncertain. This is because dY_1/dG_1 might be greater or smaller than one. In the first case, disposable income in country 1 increases, and therefore so does the demand for money: the previous analysis applies, since the upward pressure on the interest rate causes an appreciation of E which determines a decrease in Y_2. But if disposable income in country 1 goes down, there would be a downward pressure on the union interest rate and a tendency for E to depreciate: this would allow an increase in Y_2 (the same applies if disposable income in country 1 increases, but not so much that the consequent appreciation of the exchange rate overcomes the expansionary effect due to the trade linkage between country 1 and country 2).

The medium run

The same considerations apply here as for the case of monetary policy. The increase in Y_1 and the decrease in Y_2 are smaller than in the short run because of the slope of the AS curves: the change in the price level mitigates the effect of the fiscal operation on the income level. This can be checked both by inspection of the multipliers:

$$dY_1/dG_1 = \{+B_{2s}\,[P_2\,L_{2Y2}\,Y^s{}_{1P1}\,Y^s{}_{2P2} + L_2\,Y^s{}_{1P1}]\}/|D_m| > 0$$

$$dY_2/dG_1 = \{-B_{2s}\,[P_1\,L_{1Y1}\,Y^s{}_{1P1}\,Y^s{}_{2P2} + L_1\,Y^s{}_{2P2}]\}/|D_m| < 0$$

and graphically, as shown in Fig. 15 for country 1 and Fig. 16 for country 2.

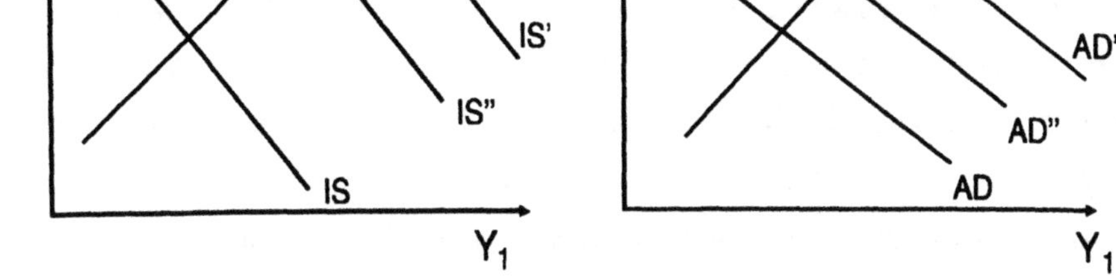

Fig. 15: The medium-run effects of an expansionary fiscal policy in country 1.

As far as country 1 is concerned, the increase in government expenditure causes a rightward shift of the IS curve to IS'.

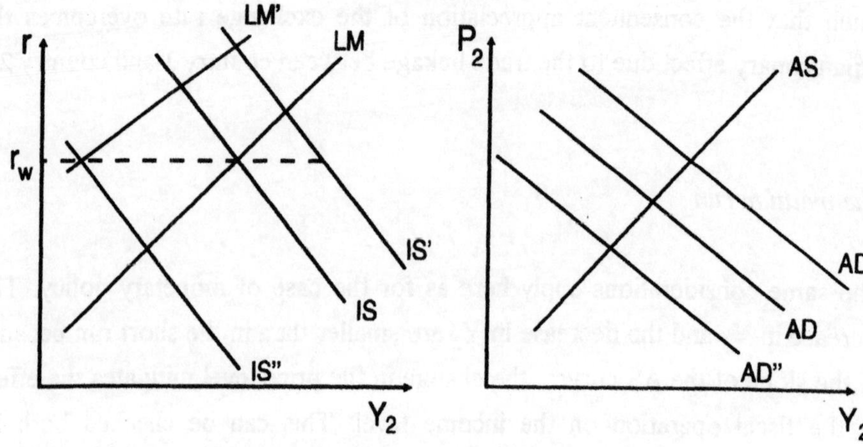

Fig. 16: The medium-run effects on country 2 of a fiscal expansion in country 1.

Also the IS curve of country 2 shifts to IS' because of the trade linkage mechanism. The AD curves of both countries shift to the right. Y_1, Y_2, P_1 and P_2 all increase. The union interest rate is now higher than the world one: E, therefore, appreciates and the loss in competitiveness, together with the increase in the price level, makes IS' shift to IS" in both countries. The overall effect on Y_1 is still positive, while that on Y_2 is contractionary, even if the effect is mitigated by the decrease of the price level with respect to the short-run case.

As for the LM curves, the final effect must be a shift to the right in country 1, due to the money inflow from country 2 after the fiscal expansion and the consequent existence of a positive interest rate differential (this is stronger than the effect of the increase in prices, which pushes the curve to the left); in country 2, instead, the final position of the LM curve will be to the left of the original one, at LM', for the converse reason.

In the case of the demand for money depending on the consumer price index rather than on the domestic price level, the same considerations as for the short-run case apply: the multipliers are not reported here for the sake of brevity, since they do not add much to the significance of the analysis.

The long run

The increase in the level of income in both the union member-countries due to an expansionary fiscal policy in one of them is the result obtained by applying the model of equations 1.1 - 1.5. In that case, the appreciation of E, making foreign goods cheaper for the union consumers, will bring about an increase in the supply of labour and therefore in the aggregate supply schedules of the union member-countries, thus strengthening the expansionary effect of the policy operation in both countries. In the long run, therefore, fiscal policy effects are of the same sign in both union member-countries. The force which drives this result is the adjustment on the supply side. One can also notice that, if the countries have symmetric reactions, the multipliers have the same value and therefore the final effect on income is the same in both members of the union:

$$dY_1/dG_1 = [(-B_{2P1/P2}Y^s{}_{1s}/P_2)(L_2+L_1P_1/P_2)]/|D_1| > 0;$$

$$dY_2/dG_1 = [(-B_{2P1/P2}Y^s{}_{1s}/P_2)(L_2+L_1P_1/P_2)]/|D_1| > 0.$$

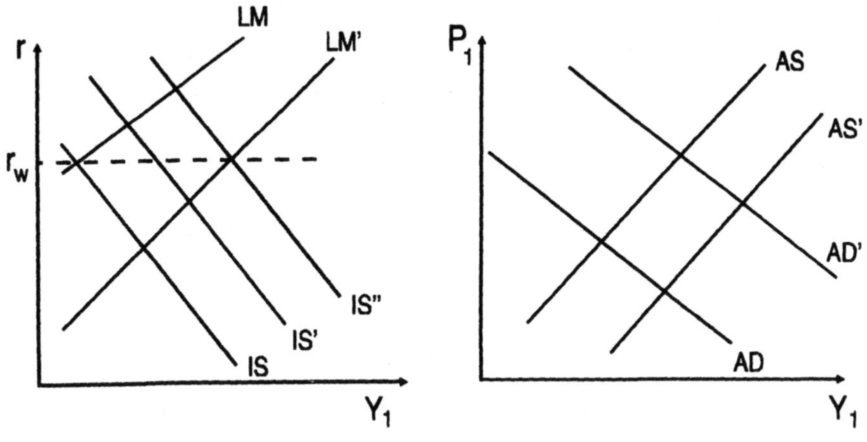

Fig. 17: The long-run effects of a fiscal expansion in country 1.

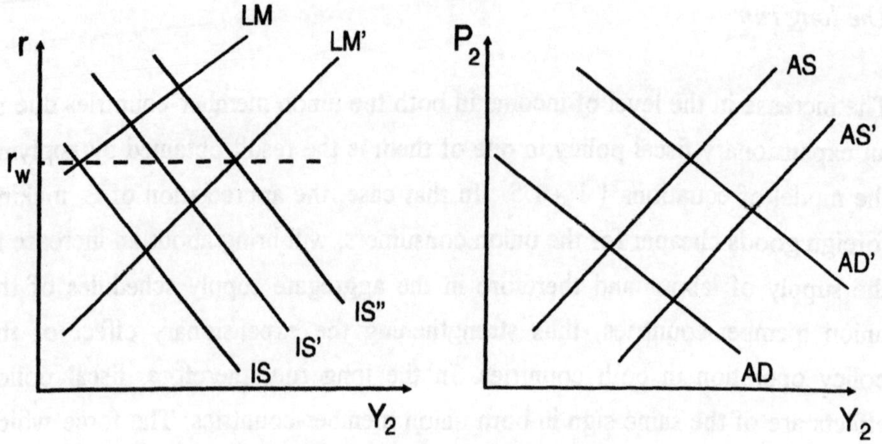

Fig. 18: The long-run effects on country 2 of a fiscal expansion in country 1.

The results can be shown also graphically (Figs. 17 and 18 for country 1 and 2 respectively): when G_1 increases, the AD curve of country 1 shifts to the right; the aggregate demand curve of country 2 shifts to the right as well because of the trade linkage mechanism. The increase in Y_1 and Y_2 causes the interest rate of the union to be above r_w; thus E appreciates. The aggregate supply curves will then shift to the right as well because of the usual assumption.

If one applies the full model, i. e. eqns. 1.1 - 1.5, with the dependence of money demand on the consumer price index and that of aggregate supply on the real exchange rate with the other union member-country, the results obtained in the previous analysis partially change (the multipliers are not reported here since they are tediously long and complex). The effect of the introduction of the consumer price index in the demand for money are as above analysed. As for the influence of the real exchange rate towards the other union member-country, the result for the country not undertaking the fiscal expansion become of ambiguous sign, as shown in Feuerstein/Siebke (1990) for the case of symmetric union member-countries. Being the nominal intra-union exchange rate irrevocably fixed, upward or downward pressures on the real one will result in a change of the ratio between the two domestic output price levels, i. e. P_2/P_1 for country 1 and P_1/P_2 for country 2. The ratio

P_2/P_1 decreases because of the money outflow from country 2 to country 1; therefore, the aggregate supply curve of country 2 shifts backwards and the final effect on its income level can be either contractionary or expansionary.

4. The model, the change in structural parameters and the optimality and existence conditions issues

The fact that policy operations affect the union member-countries in a way which depends on their characteristics (i.e. size, responsiveness of the trade balance to changes in the exchange rate, of money demand to changes in income and of aggregate supply to changes in the real exchange rate) shifts the analysis to the problem of the optimality of belonging to an exchange rate union.

The criterion of factor mobility

Mundell in his 1961 paper on the optimum size of currency areas concluded that regions should be defined on the basis of factor mobility and that single currency areas should correspond to regions, i.e. have internal factor mobility (which allows for the use of a single currency within the region) and external factor immobility (with a corresponding flexible exchange rate regime with the rest of the world).

However, the mobility of factors is not something predetermined with respect to the choice of the exchange rate system. For instance, let us consider the decision process of a labour supplier who has the possibility of changing his location from country 1 to country 2. If the present discounted value of the flow of income in 2 is bigger than that in 1, the agent will be willing to migrate. But the persistence of a positive differential is not certain. As pointed out in Bertola (1989), the higher this uncertainty is, the bigger the difference between remunerations in the two countries must be.

As long as the choice of the exchange rate regime affects the degree of uncertainty, factor mobility is a variable endogenous to the system. In the case of moving to a fixed exchange rate regime, there are two factors to be considered: (i) the variability of the nominal exchange rate is eliminated: this, of course, acts as a force reducing uncertainty and therefore enhancing mobility; (ii) the way variability of income is affected is not univocal.

One can first consider the difference between a flexible exchange rate regime and a fixed exchange rate one between two countries, 1 and 2, in the presence of a shock hitting the real sector of country 1, for instance, and shifting its IS curve to the right. The increase in income causes demand for money and therefore the interest rate to go up; it also stimulates the demand for imported goods. The overall effect on the balance of payments depends on various factors, primarily the degree of capital mobility. Assuming this is perfect, with a flexible exchange rate regime, the incipient capital inflow causes the price of the foreign currency to decrease; the subsequent decline in competitiveness shifts back the IS curve of country 1: income declines and the effect of the initial shock is therefore offset (see Fig. 19).

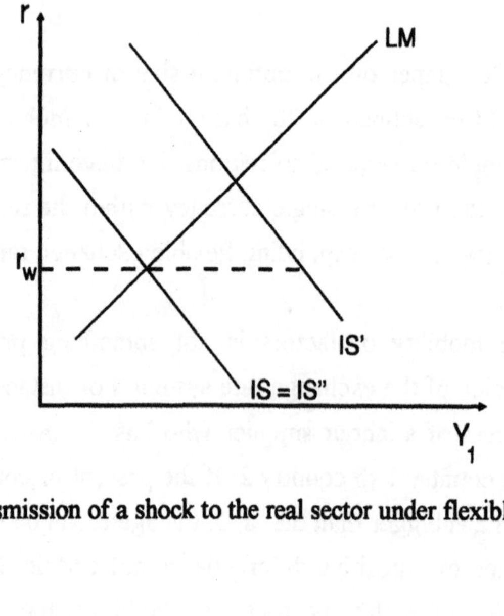

Fig. 19: The transmission of a shock to the real sector under flexible exchange rates.

With a fixed exchange rate regime, instead, the downward pressure on the exchange rate induced by the interest rate being above the world level is offset by the monetary authority through selling the domestic currency, thus increasing foreign reserves and therefore the money stock: the LM curve shifts to the right and the final effect on income is expansionary (see Fig. 20). In the presence of a real shock, therefore, fixed exchange rates involve a higher variability of income and therefore a higher degree of uncertainty.

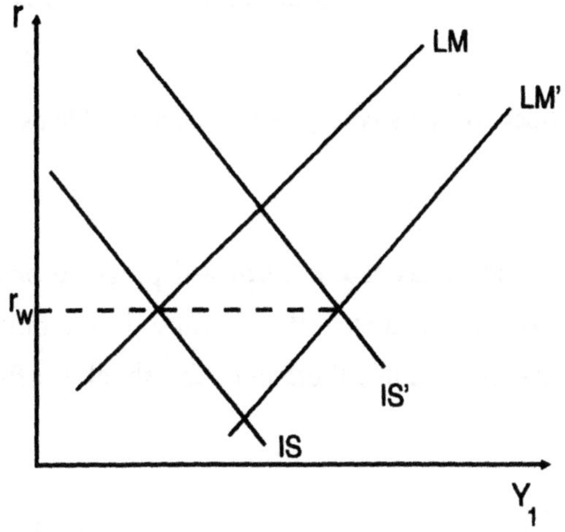

Fig. 20: The transmission of a shock to the real sector under fixed exchange rates.

The result is reversed in the presence of a shock to the monetary sector: if the LM curve of country 1 is shifted to the right, its interest rate is below the one in 2; to maintain the balance of payments equilibrium, the flexible exchange rate depreciates, thus leading to an increase in competitiveness and the outward shift of the IS curve: the level of income increases (see Fig. 21).

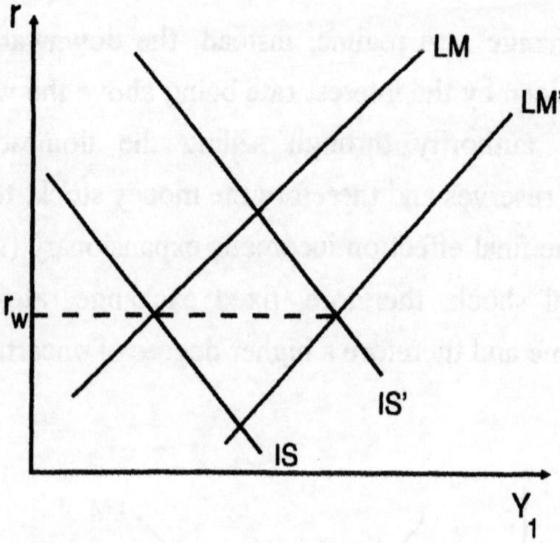

Fig. 21: A shock to the monetary sector under flexible exchange rates.

With fixed exchange rates, instead, the upward pressure on the exchange rate is neutralized, with the consequence of a decrease in the money stock: the LM curve then shifts back and the initial effect of the shock is offset (see Fig. 22).

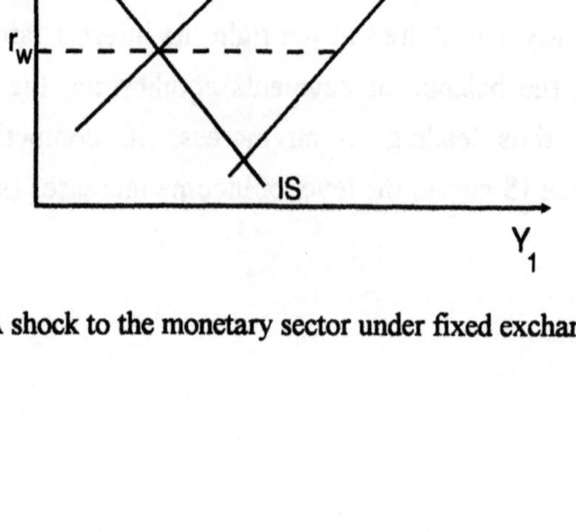

Fig. 22: A shock to the monetary sector under fixed exchange rates.

The *variability of income*, therefore, *depends on the exchange rate system* adopted. Flexible exchange rates, which directly affect competitiveness and therefore act on the IS curve, are stabilizing in response to shocks affecting the real sector; fixed exchange rates, the maintainance of which is accomplished by changes in reserves, are stabilizing when the shocks interest the LM curve.

The variability of income and uncertainty generally affect the mobility of factors, which, on its turn, can act like an adjustment mechanism, replacing the flexibility of the exchange rate. One can integrate this analysis, which considers the "world" as formed by two countries only, with the one of the three-component model presented above.

In the case of a real shock which increases Y_1 and decreases Y_2, apart from the direct effect on the level of income, there will be: as for country 1, an increase in L_1, and therefore in the rate of interest, and in the demand for imports, that partially offsets the increase in income; the opposite will happen in country 2. There will also be the changes in reserves necessary to keep the intra-union exchange rate fixed, but now one must also consider the total effect on $(Y_1 + Y_2)$and on the level of the union interest rate.

If $r > r_w$, the (flexible) exchange rate towards the rest of the world appreciates, thus leading to a rightward shift of the aggregate supply curves in the union countries. The union's income increases and, even if the precise effect in the single country is difficult to assess, the initial disequilibrium may be partially overcome also without factor mobility: Y_2 eventually increases and the price level in country 1 decreases. If the countries have the same parameters appearing in their IS, LM and AS curves and the shocks are of the same magnitudes (with opposite sign) in both countries, then the supply adjustments will offset those effects with no need for factor mobility.

As for the case of a shock in the monetary sector, which shifts the LM curve to the right, e.g. an expansion of the money stock, it has already been shown that, with integration between the security and/or the goods markets of the union member-countries, both Y_1 and Y_2 increase, in contrast with the outcome of the two-country model, but that, introducing real wage rigidities and changes in the price levels, the shock would have no (lasting) effect. The other side of this result, however, is that, in the presence of price rigidities, the speed of demand and, especially, supply adjustments might be reduced when moving to a fixed exchange rate system, thus increasing the fluctuations in the level of income.

The criterion of the degree of openness

Under a flexible exchange rate regime and a high degree of openess to international trade, a shift of demand from non-tradables to tradables causes a depreciation. The price of tradables increases and that of non-tradables decreases by the rate of depreciation. Since the ratio of the former to the latter is high, the price level increases sharply. The country under consideration, therefore, had rather adopted a fixed exchange rate regime, which is preferrable in terms of internal price stability. However, if exchange rates are fixed only with some countries, e.g. the other members of a monetary union, this stabilization goal might not be reached.

Country i's net exports in fact can be decomposed into the net exports towards the other union member-countries and those towards the rest of the world (e. g., B_1 can be decomposed in U_1 (P_2/P_1, Y_1, Y_2), net exports towards country 2, and T_1 (EP_w/P_1, Y_1, Y_w), net exports towards the rest of the world). If the sensitivity of this second part of the trade balance to changes in the exchange rate is relatively high, and goods imported from the countries not belonging to the union are a substantial share of the consumption basket, the flexibility of the exchange rate towards the rest of the world will negatively affect price stability in spite of the establishing of fixed exchange rates with the union countries.

The criterion of the degree of product diversification

Another aspect which might change during the process of formation of the monetary union, provided that this is accompanied by an economic integration process too, is the production pattern of each member country. Regions, in fact, can not be identified only on the basis of factor mobility. Another parameter is that of similarities in the goods they produce. As long as integration implies completely free circulation of goods, specialization in production is a probable outcome. This, however, will act as a factor of differentiation among "regions", and, if these coincide with the original countries, sector specific shocks will also be country specific shocks, thus introducing a disruptive force into the union.

The Phillips curve approach

In the previous analysis it has been assumed that the flexible exchange rate towards the rest of the world adjusts in order to keep the union in external balance. This is however true for the union as a whole, i. e. for the sum of country 1 and country 2 balance of payments towards the rest of the world, and does not imply that each of them is equal to zero: on the contrary, there will be a tendency for one of them to be in a deficit position and for the other one to be in a surplus one. This will exert a pressure towards a depreciation of the currency of the former, say country 1, and appreciation of that of the latter, say country 2. Being the intra-union exchange rate irrevocably fixed, however, there will be an outflow of reserves from the deficit to the surplus country, with unemployment increasing and inflation decreasing in country 1 and the opposite happening in country 2. This will push the countries away from their desired point on the Phillips curve. The distributions of the costs of the adjustment will depend on the institutional rules regulating it. In the case that unemployment is to be kept constant within the union as a whole, Fleming (1978) has demonstrated that this would imply a higher average level of inflation. The unification process itself, in conclusion, might bring about impulses which make the cohesion of the union more difficult.

Conclusions

The main results obtained with the model can be summarized as follows.

a) Effects of monetary policy in the short run.

Monetary policy is effective in the short run: an increase in the money supply of one union member-country has an expansionary effect on the income level of the whole union. The qualitative result is the same as in the traditional two-country model with fixed exchange rates. However, the mechanism operating in the latter is the redistribution of the initial increase in the money stock (because of the fixed exchange rate system and the perfect mobility of capital), which dampens the expansionary effect in the country which undertakes the monetary operation and increases it abroad; in the former, instead, the expansionary effect of monetary policy works through the responsiveness of the union member-countries trade balances to the depreciation of the exchange rate towards the rest of the world. The result differs from the case in which a country not belonging to an exchange rate union has flexible exchange rates with the other country (or rest of the world): a monetary expansion leads to an increase in income in the country which undertakes it, but to a decrease in the other one, because of the loss in competitiveness. Another conclusion to be drawn is that the (relatively) small union member-country is the one which bears the (relatively) larger effect of the adjustment process, in terms of induced increases in the income level. This is because the effect of monetary policy works through the responsiveness of the union member-countries trade balances to changes in the exchange rate towards the rest of the world. The value of this parameter is typically bigger for a small country than for a big one, because the former will be more import-oriented and less able to substitute imported goods with domestic produced ones. Another result is that the effect of monetary policy does not depend on which country undertakes the operation. However, the size of the country performing it is again relevant: the bigger the country, the bigger the effect on the union money supply and therefore on the income levels of the economies.

b) Effects of monetary policy in the medium run.

It has been shown that allowing price flexibility does not change the sign of the results obtained in the short-run framework, but that the magnitudes of the multipliers are smaller.

c) Effects of monetary policy in the long run.

Monetary policy is ineffective. The result depends on two mechanisms: the flexibility of the exchange rate towards the rest of the world and the supply-side reaction to changes in the real exchange rate. The adjustment process is therefore different from the one operating in the Mundell-Fleming two-country fixed exchange rate model, though leading to the same results, and resembles instead the flexible exchange rate and price flexibility case, because of the introduction of the rest of the world as a third component.

d) Effects of fiscal policy in the short run.

It has been shown that an increase in government expenditure has an expansionary effect on the level of income in the country which performs it, while it leads to a decrease in the level of activities in the other one. In the absence of the rest of the world as a third component, income would still increase in the first country and *might* as well fall in the second one, because of the money outflow necessary to keep the intra-union exchange rate at the fixed level. The result differs from the case in which a country not belonging to an exchange rate union has flexible exchange rates with the other country (or rest of the world): fiscal policy is expansionary also abroad, because of the home country appreciation/foreign country depreciation. It has also been shown that, in the three-country version, the overall effect on the income level of the union as a whole depends on the relative sensitivities of money demand in the two union member-countries, in the sense that total income will expand if the country which undertakes the operation has a lower responsivness.

e) Effects of fiscal policy in the medium run.

It has been shown that price flexibility dampens the induced changes in the level of activities with respect to the short-run case.

f) Effects of fiscal policy in the long run.
In the long run fiscal policy effects are of the same sign in both union member-countries if the aggregate supply curve is specified as $Y_i = Y_i\ (EP_w/P_i)$. The force which drives this result is the adjustment on the supply side. It has also been shown that, if the countries have symmetric reactions, the multipliers have the same value and therefore the final effect on income is the same in both the members of the union. The final result is again the same as in the Mundell-Fleming model. If the aggregate supply curve is instead $Y_i = Y_i\ (EP_w/P_i,\ P_j/P_i)$, then the intra-union transmission is of ambiguous sign.

g) Factor mobility.
The flexibility of the exchange rates towards the rest of the world reduces the need for factor mobility as a stabilization instrument.

h) The degree of openness.
The blocking of parities only with the other union member-countries does not guarantee the accomplishment of price stability when a flexible exchange rate system is maintained with the rest of the world.

(i) The degree of product diversification.
The unification process enhances specialization in production, thus increasing the probability of specific shocks.

(l) The Phillips curve approach.
National imbalances towards the rest of the world are a further reason why member countries could be pushed away from their Phillips curve equilibrium positions.

m) When analysing the convenience for a country to join a monetary union, one should consider that the unification process itself might bring about impulses which make cohesion more difficult.

Bibliography

Allen, P. R. (1976): "Organisation and Administration of a Monetary Union", *Princeton Studies in International Finance*, Nr. 36.

Basevi, G. (1986): "Il sistema dei cambi", in: Padoa Schioppa (ed.), *Il sistema dei cambi oggi*, Bologna.

Bertola, G. (1989): "Factor Flexibility, Uncertainty and the Exchange Rate Regimes", in: De Cecco, M.; Giovannini, G. (eds.), *A European Central Bank?*, London.

De Bonis, V. (1992): "Stabilization Policy in a Single Currency Area: An IS-LM-AS Model", in: *Quaderni del Dipartimento diEconomia*, Nr. 148, Siena.

Feuerstein, S.; Siebke, J. (1990): "Wechselkursunion und Stabilitätspolitik", in: *Zeitschrift für Wirtschafts- u. Sozialwissenschaften* 110, p. 359-379.

Feuerstein, S. (1992): *Studien zur Wechselkursunion*, Heidelberg.

Fleming, M. (1978): "On Exchange Rate Unification", in: *Essays in Economic Policy*, p. 233-260, New York.

Frenkel, J. A.; Razin, A. (1987): "The Mundell-Fleming Model A Quarter Century Later", in: *IMF Staff Papers*, Vol. 34, Nr. 4, p. 567-619.

Levin, J. H. (1983): "A Model of Stabilization Policy in a Jointly Floating Currency Area", in: Bhandari, J. S.; Putnam, B. H. (eds.), *Economic Interdependence and Flexible Exchange Rates*, Cambridge (Mass.), London, p. 329-349.

Lipsey, R. G. (1960): "The Relation between Unemployment and the Rate of Change of Money Wage Rates in the United Kingdom", 1862-1957: A Further Analysis, in: *Economica*, Vol. 27, p. 1 and following.

Mundell, R.(1961): "A Theory of Optimum Currency Areas", in: *American Economic Review*, Vol. 51, p. 657-665.

Padoa Schioppa, T. (1986): *Il sistema dei cambi oggi*, Bologna.

Phillips, A. W. (1958): "The Relationship between Unemployment and the Rate of Change of Money Wage Rates in the United Kingdom", 1861-1957, in: *Economica*, Vol. 25, p. 283.

Willet, T. D.; Tower, E. (1976): "The theory of Optimum Currency Area and Exchange Rate Flexibility", *Princeton Special Papers in International Economics*, Nr. 11.

CHAPTER III
MONETARY AND FISCAL POLICY IN A "SMALL" EXCHANGE RATE UNION
A STRATEGIC ANALYSIS

Introduction

In this chapter a model describing the strategic interactions between two countries forming an exchange rate union will be developed. The two countries are supposed to be subjected to exogenous disturbances coming from the rest of the world and pursue their targets using policy instruments, the change of which also affects the other member's targets. The system of interdependence is derived from chapter II's model, i. e. a modified version of the two-country Mundell-Fleming model as adapted to the exchange rate union case with the introduction of the third component "rest of the world" by means of exogenous variables. In particular, the medium-run version of the model will be used, as the most idoneous for the purpose of analysing policy interactions. This distinguishes the system of interdependence from the two-country ones used in the already existing literature, as, for instance, in Niehans (1968), Hamada (1974, 1976), Corden (1978).

The first part of the chapter is concerned with monetary policy. The negative result of the Danish referendum on the ratification of the treaty of Maastricht of June 2nd 1992 has given voice to the doubts and fears of this small country on the road to monetary unification with economically stronger partners. This chapter tries to give a theoretical foundation to these concerns by analysing the interdependence of the national monetary policies of two countries joining an exchange rate union. Particular attention is given to the problems of the distributions of the benefits deriving from cooperation when the two members have different economic importance. In section 1 the system of interdependence and the authorities' utility functions underlying the strategic interactions are presented. The system is then solved in section 2, where the

Nash, Stackelberg and cooperative outcomes are contrasted. Finally, section 3 elaborates the main results obtained.

In the second part of the chapter fiscal policy is analysed. Section 4 illustrates the system of interdependence and the authorities' utility functions. Section 5 presents the outcomes corresponding to the non-cooperative, cooperative and leadership solutions. The characteristics of the model and their implications for the issue of fiscal policy coordination are finally discussed in section 6. Finally, it should be noted that the results obtained in this chapter are based on static game theoretical models: a dynamic framework would lead to different conclusions about the stability of the cooperative solutions.

1. Monetary policy: the system of interdependence and the autorities' utility functions

In this section a model describing the strategic monetary policy interaction between two countries forming an exchange rate union will be presented. Each country pursues two domestic targets, output and the price level, and uses as an instrument the supply of money. When a country changes its instrument, it affects its own targets as well as those of the other member of the union. This interdependence, added to the fact that the number of targets is larger than that of available instruments, introduces scope for policy games between the two countries.

The exchange rate union does not comprehend the whole world: in addition to the two member-countries there exists a third component, the rest of the world. The exchange rate union is supposed to be so small, in an economic sense, with respect to it, that changes in its own variables do not affect those of the rest of the world, which are therefore exogenous to the model. Their changes can be treated as shocks affecting the union member-countries' economic system.

It is assumed that the model underlying such an interdependent system is similar to that developed in chapter II's. This is a three-component version of the basic Mundell-Fleming model along the lines elaborated by Levin (1983): fixed exchange rates between the two union member-countries are combined with flexible ones towards the rest of the world; perfect capital mobility is assumed both within the union and between the union and the rest of the world. The effect of a monetary expansion on the income levels of both union members is positive and its magnitude is independent of the country undertaking the operation. The first characteristic depends on the responsiveness of the trade balance to changes in the exchange rate towards the rest of the world: the monetary expansion causes a downward pressure on the union interest rate and therefore the flexible exchange rate towards the rest of the world depreciates, thus improving the trade balance and income. As for the second characteristics, in each country the effect of the operation is the same whatever union member has undertaken it, since, given the constraint imposed by the fixity of the intra-union exchange rate and the full mobility of capital, the money supply is unique for the whole union.

One can therefore write the following reduced form equations:

(1) $$dy_1 = a_1 dm_1 + b_1 dm_2 + c_1 dz,$$

(2) $$dy_2 = a_2 dm_2 + b_2 dm_1 + c_2 dz,$$

(3) $$dp_1 = i_1 dm_1 + j_1 dm_2 + g_1 dz,$$

(4) $$dp_2 = i_2 dm_2 + j_2 dm_1 + g_2 dz,$$

where:

dm_i = change in country i's domestic credit;
dp_i = change in country i's price level;
dy_i = change in country i's output;
dz = shock originating from the rest of the world;

and the subscripts "i" = 1 for the union member-country 1, 2 for the union member-country 2 and w for the rest of the world.

Equation (1) shows that a change in country 1's level of output can be induced by a change in the money supply of either union member-country and by a shock originating from the rest of the world. The underlying model says that the effect of a change in the money supply on country 1's output is positive and has the same magnitude whatever union member undertakes the operation, i. e.:

$$a_1 = b_1 > 0.$$

The same considerations apply to country 2. Equation (3) describes how a change in country 1's price of domestic output can be induced by a change in either member-countries' money supply and by a shock originating from the rest of the world. From the underlying model one obtains that:

$$i_1 = j_1 > 0.$$

The same is true for country 2. If one is interested in the consumer price index (q_i) rather than in the price of domestic output, equations (3) and (4) must be replaced by:

(3') $$dq_1 = w_1 dm_1 + l_1 dm_2 + f_1 dz,$$

(4') $$dq_2 = w_2 dm_2 + l_2 dm_1 + f_2 dz.$$

The consumer price index, q_i, is a weighted average of the prices of domestic and foreign products, the weights being the propensities to consume out of domestic and foreign goods. Therefore, q_1 will be expressed by the following equation:

(5) $$q_1 = \mu_1 p_2 + \mu_2 (e - p_w) + (1 - \mu_1 - \mu_2) p_1,$$

where:

$$1 > \mu_1, \mu_2 > 0.$$

Changes in q_1 can derive from a change either in p_1 or in p_2 or in e. Changes in prices are described by equations (3) and (4). Changes in the exchange rate towards the rest of the world (de) are caused by changes in the money supply of either union member-country or by a shock coming from the rest of the world, as equation (6) describes:

$$(6) \qquad de = tdm_1 + kdm_2 + vdz, \qquad t = k > 1, v > 1.$$

Substituting in (5) from (3), (4) and (6) one obtains:

$$(7)\ dq_1 = (1\text{-}\mu_1\text{-}\mu_2)(i_1dm_1 + j_1dm_2 + g_1dz) + \mu_1(i_2dm_2 + j_2dm_1 + g_2dz) + \mu_2(tdm_1 + kdm_2 + vdz),$$

which can also be written:

$$(8)\ dq_1 = [(1\text{-}\mu_1\text{-}\mu_2)i_1 + \mu_1 j_2 + \mu_2 t]dm_1 + [1\text{-}\mu_1\text{-}\mu_2)j_1 + \mu_1 i_2 + \mu_2 k]dm_2 + [(1\text{-}\mu_1\text{-}\mu_2)g_1 + \mu_1 g_2 + \mu_2 v]dz.$$

Putting:

$$[(1\text{-}\mu_1\text{-}\mu_2)i_1 + \mu_1 j_2 + \mu_2 t] = w_1,$$

$$[1\text{-}\mu_1\text{-}\mu_2)j_1 + \mu_1 i_2 + \mu_2 k] = l_1,$$

$$[(1\text{-}\mu_1\text{-}\mu_2)g_1 + \mu_1 g_2 + \mu_2 v] = f_1,$$

one obtains equation (3') and symmetrically for country 2 and equation (4'). From these operations and the underlying model one obtains that:

$$w_i = l_i > 0.$$

The next step is to introduce the policymakers' preferences. It is assumed that policymakers dislike changes in the output level and in the consumer price index of their own country, i. e. that they maximize the following utility functions:

(9) $$U_1 = -\frac{1}{2}\,[h\,(dy_1)^2 + (dq_1)^2],$$

(10) $$U_2 = -\frac{1}{2}\,[h\,(dy_2)^2 + (dq_2)^2].$$

In the case of a complete monetary union, as opposed to an exchange rate union, one cannot distinguish between dm_1 and dm_2, since a unique central bank and therefore a unique money supply exist. In such a case, a weighted sum of the utility functions of the members is being maximized, the weight generally depending on each country's relative economic importance.

2. Monetary policy: the Nash, cooperative, Stackelberg and monetary union solutions

In this section the system presented in section 1 will be solved. In order to do this, one must first substitute for dy_1, from equation (1), and dq_1, from equation (3'), into equation (9), thus obtaining:

(11) $$U_1 = -\frac{1}{2}\,[h\,(a_1dm_1 + b_1dm_2 + c_1dz)^2 + (w_1dm_1 + l_1dm_2 + f_1dz)^2].$$

Equation (11) is the formula for the authorities' utility functions. Substituting in from the constraints, one obtains:

(12) $$U_1 = -\frac{1}{2}\,[h\,(a_1^2dm_1^2 + b_1^2dm_2^2 + c_1^2dz^2 + 2a_1dm_1b_1dm_2 + 2a_1dm_1c_1dz + 2b_1dm_2c_1dz) + (w_1^2dm_1^2 + l_1^2dm_2^2 + f_1^2dz^2 + 2w_1dm_1l_1dm_2 + 2w_1dm_1f_1dz + 2l_1dm_2f_1dz)].$$

If one differentiates it with respect to dm_1 and equates to zero, one finds the first order condition for an optimum in country 1:

(13) $$dU_1/dm_1 = -\,[(ha_1^2 + w_1^2)dm_1 + (ha_1b_1 + w_1l_1)dm_2 + (ha_1c_1 + w_1f_1)dz = 0.$$

Equation (13) can be written so as to show the reaction function of country 1, i. e. the optimal value of dm_1 for a given value of dm_2 (and for a given value of the shock dz):

$$(14) \quad dm_1 = -[(ha_1b_1 + w_1l_1)dm_2 + (ha_1c_1 + w_1f_1)dz]/(ha_1^2 + w_1^2).$$

This is country 1's reaction function, R_1, which is downward sloping in the (dm_1, dm_2) space because of the positive spillover effect existing between the two union member-countries: both dm_1 and dm_2 affect y_1 and q_1 according to a positive relationship; therefore, other things being equal, an increase in m_1 must be counteracted by a decrease in m_2 if the country maximizes its utility. Making use of the result that $a_1 = b_1$ and $w_1 = l_1$, the equation for R_1 becomes:

$$(14') \quad dm_1 = -[(\beta a_1^2 + w_1^2)/(\beta a_1^2 + w_1^2)]dm_2 + [(\beta a_1c_1 + w_1f_1)/(\beta a_1^2 + w_1^2)]dz.$$

Its slope is therefore equal to - 1.

Applying the same procedure to country 2, one obtains:

$$(15) \quad dm_2 = -[(\beta a_2^2 + w_2^2)/(\beta a_2^2 + w_2^2)]dm_1 + [(\beta a_2c_2 + w_2f_2)/(\beta a_2^2 + w_2^2)]dz,$$

which is the reaction function for country 2, R_2, the slopes of which is also equal to -1. If country 1 and country 2 are "mirror images", it will also be true that:

$$a_1 = a_2,$$
$$c_1 = c_2,$$
$$w_1 = w_2,$$
$$f_1 = f_2,$$

and therefore the two reaction functions will also have the same intercept. This means that the lines representing them coincide (see Fig. 1). The system does not give a unique non-cooperative solution in this case, the Nash equilibrium points being infinite and corresponding to the points of the $R_1 = R_2$ line.

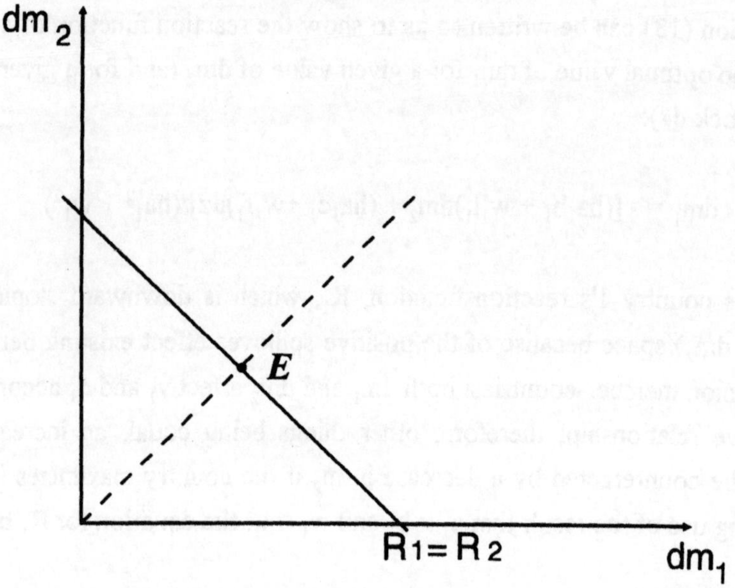

Fig. 1: The "degenerated" monetary policy game with symmetric union member-countries.

If the two member countries differ from each other in the relevant parameters, then the intercepts of R_1 and R_2 will not be the same and the two reaction functions, instead of coinciding, will be two parallel lines (see Fig. 2). In this case, the system does not have a non-cooperative solution.

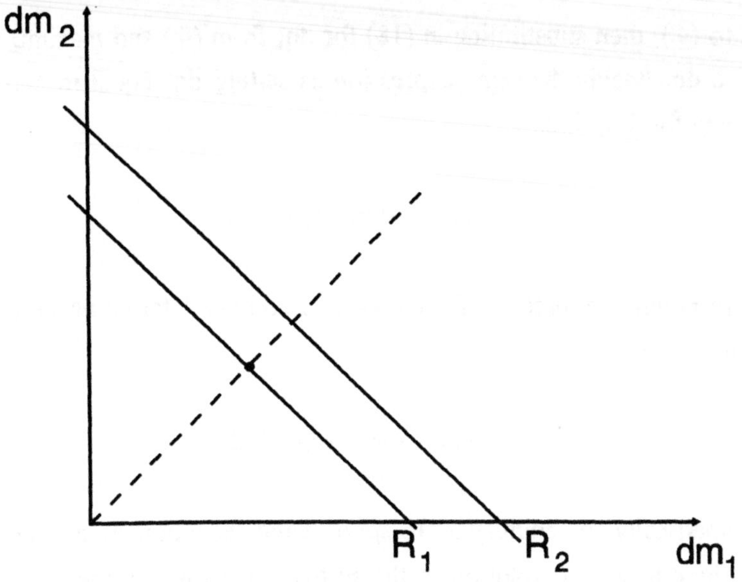

Fig. 2: The lack of a Nash equilibrium in the monetary policy game when the member countries differ from each other.

These situations are a reflection of the loss of monetary autonomy deriving from joining an exchange rate union in the presence of perfect capital mobility. In the first case, imposing the condition $dm_1 = dm_2$, point E in Fig. 1 becomes a sustainable outcome, since it belongs to both reaction functions. Accordingly, there is no combination of dm_1 and dm_2 such that the countries can obtain their bliss points in the presence of a shock, since they act like a unique instrument, making it impossible to achieve the two targets. The following system:

(16) $$a_1 dm_1 + a_1 dm_2 + c_1 dz = 0$$

(17) $$w_1 dm_1 + w_1 dm_2 + f_1 dz = 0$$

cannot give a solution for dm_1 and dm_2. If a country has only one target in its objective function, instead, then its reaction function also defines its bliss points. For instance, if country 1 maximizes

(18) $$U_1 = - \tfrac{1}{2}\,(dq_1)^2$$

subject to (4'), then substituting in (18) for dq_1 from (4') and maximizing with rispect to dm_1 yields the same expression as setting dq_1 equal to zero in (4') and solving for dm_1, i. e.:

(19) $$dm_1 = -dm_2 -(f_1/w_1)dz.$$

The corresponding expression for the case of country 1 targeting only income would be:

(19') $$dm_1 = -dm_2 -(c_1/az1)dz$$

and symmetrically for country 2. In spite of the reduction of the number of targets, there is still no solution to the system, as shown by the fact that the two reaction functions, loci of the bliss points, are parallel or coincide (in the case of the two countries being mirror images and targeting the same variable. However, it is now possible to define imperialistic solutions (even if not a unique one). This corresponds to the case of the country which has reduced the number of targets to one, or one of them if both have done it, imposing the values of dm_1 and dm_2 corresponding to one point on its reaction function onto the other. The former country will then achieve its bliss. In the special case of the country being mirror images and targeting the same variable, each combination of dm_1 and dm_2 belonging to their coinciding reaction functions will grant them with the highest possible utility (see Fig. 3).

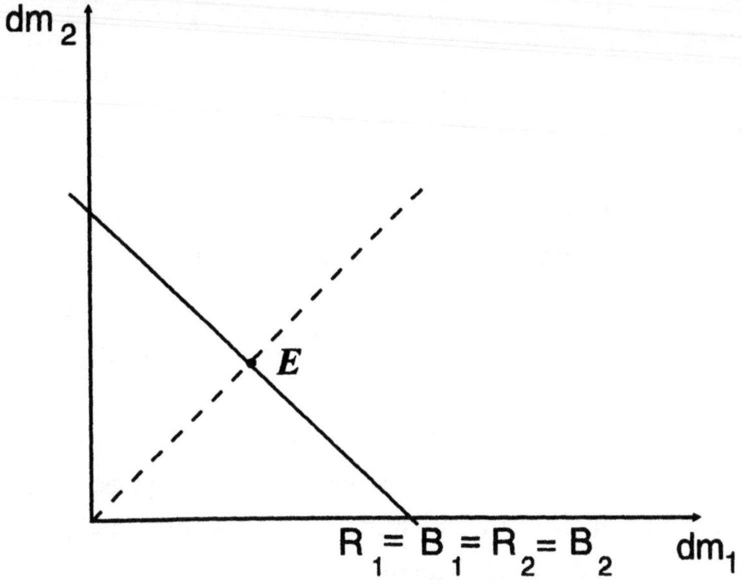

Fig. 3: The achievement of the bliss by symmetric member countries targeting one variable only.

Apart from these particular cases, these situations call for the creation of a central monetary authority for the union as a whole and therefore, to conclude, the solution for a full monetary union, i. e. for the case in which there is only one monetary institution and therefore only one instrument for the union as a whole, will be analysed. It would not be correct to speak of coordination for this situation, since decisions are taken by a single subject and concern the unique dm. In this case, the system of macroeconomic interdependence for the two union member-countries is the following:

(20) $$dy_1 = a_1\, dm + c_1\, dz$$

(21) $$dy_2 = a_2\, dm + c_2\, dz$$

(22) $$dq_1 = w_1\, dm + f_1\, dz$$

(23) $$dq_2 = w_2\, dm + f_2\, dz$$

where :

$$dm = dm_1 + dm_2.$$

The union's monetary authority maximizes a weighted sum of equations (9) and (10), the weights being β_1 and β_2, summing up to unity.

(24) $$U_u = - \beta_1 [h(dy_1)^2 + (dq_1)^2] - \beta_2 [h(dy_2)^2 + (dq_2)^2].$$

Maximizing equation (24) over dm subject to equations (20) - (23) yields the following value for the change in the instrument in response to a negative shock originating in the rest of the world for the case of β_1 and β_2 being both equal to ½ and h_1 and h_2 both equal to h:

(25) $$dm = \{[(ha_1c_1 + w_1f_1) + (ha_2c_2 + w_2f_2)]/[(ha_1^2 + c_1^2) + (ha_2^2 + c_2^2)]\}dz.$$

3. Concluding remarks on monetary policy coordination

The differences between the present analysis and other strategic models of monetary policy coordination, e. g. those in Canzoneri/Henderson (1988) and Fratianni/von Hagen (1990a), derive from the underlying system of interdependence. That adopted here is derived from chapter II's model and has therefore three main distinguishing features: a) the constraints imposed by the monetary operations of one union member-country on the other one are positive, while the EMS models existing in the literature have negative ones; this derive from the positive values of the domestic income multiplier of foreign monetary policy; b) the member countries are not assumed to be mirror images, so that the question of the convenience of belonging to the union can be addressed with respect to the countries' characteristics, e. g. the economic dimension; this is made possible by the fact that the multipliers of the underlying model are derived without the use of symmetry assumptions; c) the shocks which start the policy games are not undefined world shocks, but changes in the rest of the world economic variables; this is because the underlying model is not a two-country model, but a three-component one, with the rest of the world economic variables exogenously affecting the "small" union ones.

More in particular, a game theoretical representation of the inconsistency of autonomus national monetary policies in a regime of (irrevocably) fixed exchange rates and perfect capital mobility has been presented. In such a situation, a "solution" can be reached either if one country, which targets only one variable, is able of imposing the combination of dm_1 and dm_2 corresponding to one of its bliss points to the othe country or if the countries, recognizing that the monetary instrument is unique, agree to maximize a weighted sum of their objective functions over it.

The relative size of the weight represents the country's "share" in the distribution of the benefits deriving from the joint reaction to the shock. In particular, it is plausible to think that a general criterion might be that of assigning a smaller weight to the utility functions of countries of minor economic importance. This can explain the doubts of a small country about the convenience of joining a monetary union with much stronger partners and its threat of leaving it unless a larger weight is awarded to it. This might involve, if the big country has an interest in the survival of the union itself, that a small country will tendencially obtain a greater weight within the common institutions than that corresponding to its real economic dimension.

The situation is even worse if the small and the big country have a strong preference for different targets; this kind of problem, however, arises also for equally sized countries: if one member strongly dislikes changes in the price level relatively to those in output and the opposite is true for the other one, then each of them may doubt the convenience of joining the union or at least fight for the preferred variable to be given a larger weight at the union level.

4. Fiscal policy: the system of interdependence and the authorities' utility functions

In this section the fiscal policy strategic interactions between two countries forming an exchange rate union will be developed on the basis of the system of interdependence of chapter II's model. The union economic variables are therefore assumed to be dependent also on rest of the world variables. These must be considered exogenous, since the union is too small to affect them. A flexible exchange rate regime with the rest of the world and full capital mobility both within the union and between this and the rest of the world are assumed.

Each country targets income and the trade balance by using one instrument, government expenditure. The change of the instrument affects not only the country's income and trade balance, but also those of the other union member-country: the copresence of these two conditions,, i. e. a higher number of targets than of available instruments and the interdependence between the two countries, allows scope for policy games.

The system of interdependence can be represented by the following reduced form equations:

(26) $$dy_1 = a_1\, dg_1 - b_1\, dg_2 + l_1\, dz$$

(27) $$dy_2 = a_2\, dg_2 - b_2\, dg_1 + l_2\, dz$$

(28) $$dT_1 = - h_1\, dg_1 - k_2\, dg_2 + c_1\, dz$$

(29) $$dT_2 = - h_2\, dg_2 - k_1\, dg_1 + c_2\, dz$$

where dg_i indicates the change in the level of government expenditure in country i, T_i the trade balance of country i and the rest of the notation has the usual meaning. The parameters are all positive and the sign of the relationships between the instruments and the targets is derived from chapter II's model: the increase in government expenditure in one of the union member-countries causes an increase in its income level and, through the trade linkage mechanism, also in that of the other partner. Moreover, given the union money supply, the higher levels of income imply an excess demand for money with respect to the original equilibrium. The upward pressure on the rate of interest and the capital inflow can be offset by an appreciation of the exchange rate towards the rest of the world. Income will therefore decline in both union member-countries because of the loss in competitiveness and the final effect on the country not undertaking the operation will be contractionary. In particular, the effects on each member country's income level of an increase of its own government expenditure and of an increase of the partner's government expenditure will be the same in absolute value. It also follows that the effect of a fiscal expansion on the own trade balance is negative. These relationships are illustrated by equations (26) - (29).

Equation (26) says that a change in country 1's income level can be induced by a change in country 1's level of government expenditure, the sign of the relation being positive, by a change in country 2's level of government expenditure, the sign of the relation being negative, and by a change in a rest of the world variable, which is treated here as a shock. The same applies to equation (27), which refers to country 2. Equations (28) and (29) are derived as follows: T_1 can be decomposed into its two components, T_{12}, the trade balance with country 2, and T_{1w}, the trade balance with the rest of the world. In the same way T_2 can be decomposed into T_{21} and T_{2w}, with T_{12} being equal to - T_{21}. Therefore:

(30) $$dT_1 = dT_{12} + dT_{1w}$$

(31) $$dT_2 = dT_{21} + dT_{2w}$$

(32) $$dT_{12} = - dT_{21}.$$

Changes in the trade balance between country 1 and country 2 are induced by changes in the level of government spending in either country, while the trade balance with the rest of the world is affected by changes in the domestic instrument and by shocks originating in the rest of the world:

(33) $$dT_{12} = - k_1' \, dg_1 + k_2' \, dg_2 \qquad (= - dT_{21})$$

(34) $$dT_{1w} = - f_1 \, dg_1 - k_2'' \, dg_2 + c_1 \, dz$$

(35) $$dT_{2w} = - f_2 \, dg_2 - k_1'' \, dg_1 + c_2 \, dz.$$

Using these relations and putting:

$$-(k_1 + f_1) = -h_1$$
$$-(k_2 + f_2) = -h_2$$
$$-(k_2'' - k_2') = -k_2$$
$$-(k_1'' - k_1') = -k_1$$

eqations (28) and (29) are obtained. The next step is to introduce the authorities' utility functions. It is assumed that both countries dislike changes in the income level and in the trade balance, so that their utility functions take the form:

(36) $$U_1 = -1/2\,[(dy_1)^2 + \beta\,(dT_1)^2]$$

(37) $$U_2 = -1/2\,[(dy_2)^2 + \beta\,(dT_2)^2].$$

Each country, therefore, uses its instrument to counteract fluctuations in output and in the balance of trade, i. e. equation (36) is maximized over dg_1 subject to equations (26) and (28), while equation (37) is maximized over dg_2 subject to equations (27) and (29).

5. Fiscal policy: the Nash, cooperative and Stackelberg solutions

The system formed by equations (26) - (37) will now be solved and three possible types of equilibria will be analysed: the Nash, or non-cooperative, equilibrium solution, with each country selecting the value of its own instrument given the choice of the other one; the Pareto, or cooperative, equilibrium solution, with the two countries finding an agreement to maximize their utilities; the Stackelberg, or leadership, equilibrium solution, with one country acting as a leader and the other one as a follower.

In order to do this, one must substitute in equation (36) for dy_1 from equation (26) and for dT_1 from equation (28), maximize over dg_1 and set the derivative equal to zero, thus obtaining the reaction function for country 1, R_1:

$$(38)\ dg_1 = [(a_1 b_1 - ß h_1 k_2)/(a_1^2 + ß h_1^2)]\ dg_2 - [(a_1 l_1 - ß h_1 c_1)/(a_1^2 + ß h_1^2)\ dz.$$

Symmetrically, maximizing equation (37) over dg_2 substituting in for dy_2 and dT_2 from the constraints (27) and (29) yields the reaction function for country 2, R_2:

$$(39)\ dg_2 = [(a_2 b_2 - ß h_2 k_1)/(a_2^2 + ß h_2^2)]\ dg_1 - [(a_2 l_2 - ß h_2 c_2)/(a_2^2 + ß h_2^2)\ dz.$$

In the absence of a shock, each country can reach its targets by setting the change in government expenditure level equal to zero. If the countries are hit by a shock originating from the rest of the world, instead, this is no longer true. The situation can be represented in the (dg_2, dg_1) space: the reaction functions are then positively sloped, at least if ß is not too big: given the size of the shock, since dg_1 affects y_1 positively while dg_2 is linked to it by an inverse relationship, if dg_2 increases, there will be a negative dy_1 and therefore dg_1 must increase to counteract it, in order to maximize utility. The symmetric case applies to country 2. In the case of a negative shock, the intercept of R_1 with the dg_1 axis, obtained by putting $dg_2 = 0$ in equation (38), is positive and equal to $[(a_1 l_1 - ß h_1 c_1)/(a_1^2 + ß h_1^2)]\ dz$. The same applies to country 2.

The utility functions have the form of ellipses. The bliss points of the authorities are found by solving the system of equations (26) and (28) for country 1 and (27) and (29) for country 2 putting dy_i and dT_i equal to zero. The coordinates of country 1's bliss point, B_1, will then be:

$$(40)\quad dg_1 = - \{(b_1/a_1)\ [(h_1 l_1 - a_1 k_2 c_1)/(k_2 a_1 - h_1 b_1)]+(l_1 a_1)\}\ dz$$

$$(41)\qquad dg_2 = - [(h_1 l_1 - a_1 k_2 c_1)/(a_1 k_2 - h_1 b_1)].$$

The position of the bliss point depends on the relative size of the parameters describing the efficacy of a change in government expenditure and of a shock on Y_1 and B_1. For instance, if the two member countries are mirror images and c_1 and c_2 both equal to zero, then dg_1 would be positive and dg_2 negative, with dg_2 greater than dg_1 in absolute level, since in this way country 1 could obtain an increase in its income level and the positive effect of the foreign contraction on the trade balance would counteract the negative one coming from the domestic fiscal expansion.

The last thing to do in order to be able to represent this system by a diagram is to establish the position of the intersection point between the two reaction functions, *N*, which is done by solving the system formed by equations (38) and (39). This yields the following coordinates:

(42) $$dg_1 = - [(\mu_{11}\, \mu_{22} + \mu_{12})/(1 - \mu_{21}\, \mu_{11})]\, dz > 0$$

(43) $$dg_2 = - [(\mu_{21}\, \mu_{12} + \mu_{22})/(1 - \mu_{11}\, \mu_{21})]\, dz > 0$$

where:

$$\mu_{11} = (a_1\, b_1 + \beta\, h_1\, k_2)/(a_1^{\,2} + \beta\, h_1^{\,2})$$
$$\mu_{12} = (a_1\, l_1 - \beta\, h_1\, c_1)/(a_1^{\,2} + \beta\, h_1^{\,2})$$
$$\mu_{21} = (a_2\, b_2 + \beta\, h_2\, k_1)/(a_2^{\,2} + \beta\, h_2^{\,2})$$
$$\mu_{22} = (a_2\, l_2 - \beta\, h_2\, c_2)/(a_2^{\,2} + \beta\, h_2^{\,2}).$$

The coordinates are positive on the usual assumption that $h_1 > k_2$ and $h_2 > k_1$. At this point one can draw three figures, corresponding to three possible cases: Fig. 4, with *N* being on the 45° line; Fig. 5, with *N* being above it; and Fig. 6, with *N* below it.

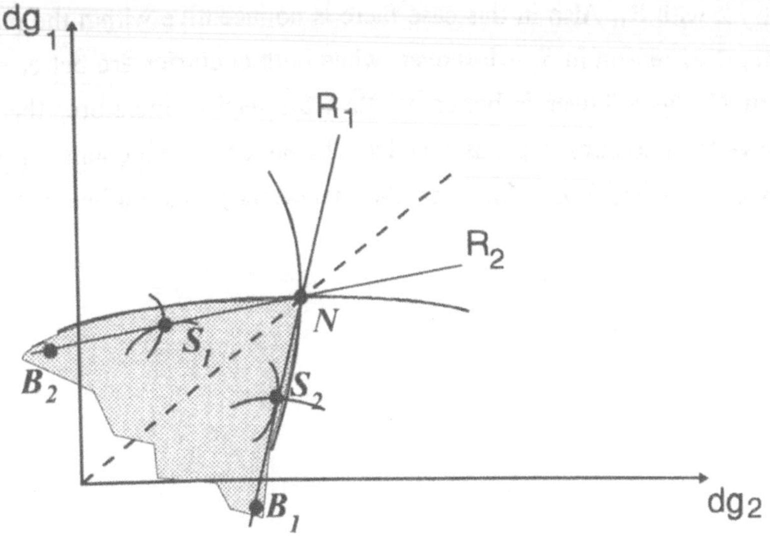

Fig. 4: The Nash, cooperative and Stackelberg solutions in the fiscal policy game with symmetric member countries.

Fig. 4 shows the symmetric case: R_1 and R_2 have equal intercepts and reciprocal slopes, with the intersection point on the 45° line. The Nash solution corresponds to point *N*: this is a Pareto inferior point, since both countries could be better off by expanding less or even by contracting. The reason for this result is that the race to contract less than the other in the end brings about an expansionary spiral.

If the two countries agree to cooperate and therefore expand less or contract, they will end up in a more favourable situation, the cooperative solution being somewhere in the shaded area, which contains all the Pareto improving points, on the contract curve, which contains the bliss points and the tangency points between the indifference curves (Pareto efficient points). The problem with this solution, apart from the difficulties in agreeing on the distributions of the benefits deriving from it, is that at least one country will then be off its reaction function and will therefore find it convenient to cheat, provided that the other one sticks to the agreement. As for the Stackelberg solution, assuming that country 2 acts as a leader, it will correspond to point S_2, i. e. the point of tangency of the possible highest indifference curve of country 2 with R_1. Also in this case there is no incentive within the model for country 2 to remain in S_2. Moreover, while both countries are better off in S_2 than in N, the follower is better off than the leader: therefore, there is no incentive for a country to act as a leader. The same is true if country 1 acts as a leader and country 2 as a follower, the Stackelberg solution being then point S_1.

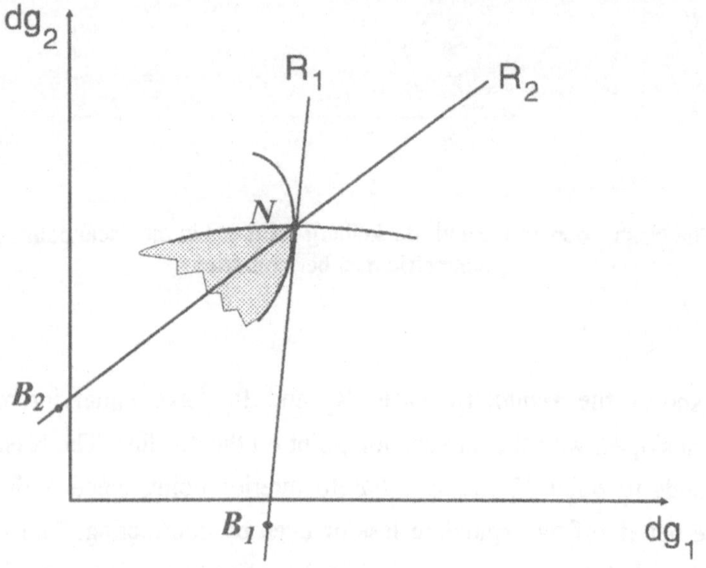

Fig. 5: In the case of country 2 being relatively more sensitive to changes in the partner's instrument, cooperation calls for country 1 expanding less.

Fig. 5 illustrates the case of N being above the 45° line. This is the case if country 2 is relatively more sensitive to changes in the other country's instrument, with a_1 being greater than b_2. In this case cooperation calls for country 1 tendencially expanding even less (or contracting even more): this is a nice correspondence with the fact that in this situation a fiscal expansion in country 1 is contractionary for the union as a whole, while the opposite is true for a contractionary policy operation.

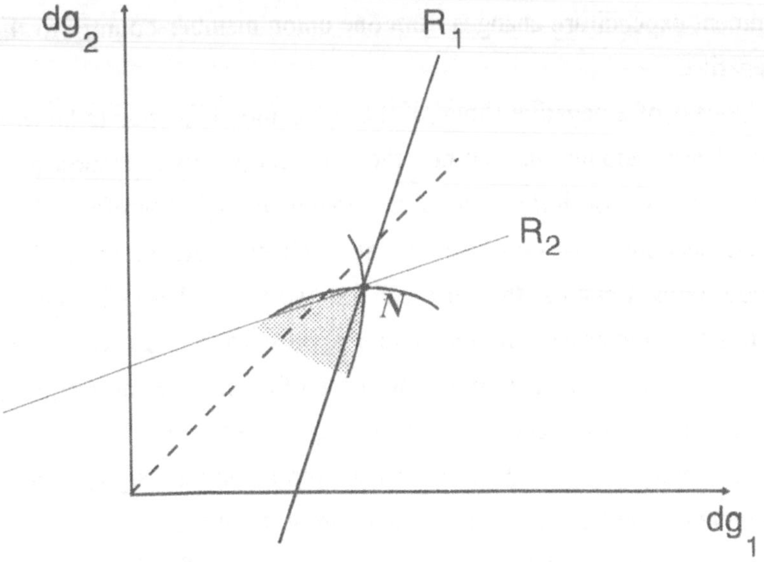

Fig. 6: In the case of country 1 being relatively more sensitive to changes in the partner's instrument, cooperation calls for country 2 expanding less.

Finally, Fig. 6 shows the opposite case, for which the same kind of explanation applies.

6. Concluding remarks on fiscal policy coordination

The results obtained in the previous section are different from those of the existing EMS models, in particular the one in de Grauwe (1990). Once again, such differences derive from the fact that the reduced form equations are derived from chapter II's model and not from the traditional Mundell-Fleming one and can be identified in the following ones.

a) There is no ambiguity as for the slopes of the reaction functions, which are unambiguously positive since the fiscal policy spillover effects are unambiguously negative (unless the consumer price index is used in the LM curve instead of the domestic price level). This is a consequence of the introduction of the rest of the world as third component of the model and therefore of the exchange rate effect, which makes the transmission of government expenditure changes from one union member-country to the other one negative.

b) In the case of a negative shock, if the authorities' bliss points lie to the left of the Nash equilibrium point, the non-cooperative response is too expansionary, not too little as in the de Grauwe model. Therefore, the system of interdependence corresponding to an exchange rate union with flexible exchange rates towards the rest of the world implies that government expenditure is increased too much in response to a negative shock. This confirms the usual result that, in the presence of a negative constraint imposed by one country's instrument to the other one, cooperation calls for doing less. In the case analysed, it might even call for the countries varying the level of government expenditure in the same direction of the shock

At this point the question of the necessity for fiscal policies to be harmonized/coordinated within an exchange rate union must be briefly addressed. The term harmonization refers to the equalization of the rules governing fiscal intervention (e. g. the same type of taxes with equal coefficients and base of imposition in all union member-countries - for direct taxation see Paladini (1992)). With particular reference to the European monetary unification process, it has been said that budgetary rules should be made uniform in order to prevent countries to follow policies leading to excessive, prolonged deficits, and therefore to the accumulation of huge public debts, to be financed by attracting capital from the other member countries by means of increased interest rates, thus exerting an upward pressure also on the interest rates of the whole Community and crowding out investment. Moreover, the need for harmonization is also induced by the possibility that these countries could increase their deficits and debts even more than they would have done if they had not been member of the Community, with the hope that the latter would eventually bail them out in spite of the non-monetary-financing committment (for this moral hazard problem see Fratianni/von Hagen (1990b)). The European Community has chosen to overcome these problems by imposing criteria for admittance to the last stage of the unification process, which should bring to the creation of the European System of Central Banks (ESCB) and the irrevocable locking of parities. There are therefore four conditions: 1) the inflation rate must not exceed the inflation rate of the three best performing member countries in terms of consumer price index stability by more than 1,5%; 2) the exchange rate shall have respected the normal fluctuations margins without severe tensions for the two preceding years; 3) the long-term nominal interest rate on government bonds pertaining to the year before the examination must not exceed the long-term interest rate of the three best performing member countries in terms of price stability by more than 2%; 4) actual or planned government deficit must not be over 3% of GDP, public debt must not exceed 60% of GDP.

However, there are several arguments against the necessity of fiscal harmonization. If capital mobility is high also between the Community and the rest of the world, the demand for savings would be met not only by the European, but by the whole world supply, thus reducing the interest rate rise and consequent crowding out effects (see Siebke (1992)). Moreover, as pointed out in Willms (1990), the market itself might offset the incentive for higher deficits, by means of larger risk premia as well as of intertemporal budget constraints. The main argument against harmonization in general is, however, that it takes away the possibility for a country to react to a shock which is specific to it and not common to the other union members. Eichengreen (1991) illustrates the case of an appreciation of the real exchange rate. Since the exchange rate is the relative price between tradables and non tradables, the relative price of the former will consequently decrease, thus leading to a reduction of supply and employment in the regions specialized in the production of tradables. The traditional political answer would be to increase the money supply in order to make the exchange rate depreciate, but this option is not available for a member of a single currency area. If fiscal policies are harmonized, also this instrument cannot be used any more for stabilization purposes. Apart from the fact that a fiscal expansion could even worsen the appreciation problem, the question is whether, even in the absence of harmonization, independent fiscal policies could still be possible: an increase in fiscal expenditure means a future increase in taxes, which could push the footloose factors of production to migrate towards other union member-country(ies) offering a better treatment.

These problems do not necessarily arise in the case of coordination, since this does not imply that all the member countries act symmetrically, e. g. in response to a shock. This term, in fact, refers to the situation in which the presence of spillover effects imposed by the policy operations of one country on the other one is taken into account, so that a position of higher economic welfare may be reached. The model presented in the previous sections has shown that this might be true for the case of an exchange rate union, but that rules concerning the division of benefits as well as a system of incentives/punishments must be drawn to accomplish and substain a cooperative outcome.

Vaubel (1978) points out that the mistrust in the ability of the national authorities to internalize the reciprocal spillover effects may call for some form of centralization. The experience of existing federal states, where national fiscal autonomy is compatible with currency unification, is actually correlated to the existence of a federal budget which represents a consistent share of GDP. This acts as a stabilizer of interregional disequilibria, since a region automatically pays less taxes and receives more social security benefits when its level of capacity utilization decreases. This stabilizing effect would be even larger if explicit provision is made for regional policy (see Campa (1989)). Cesarano (1987) points out that the number of available instruments would be smaller with respect to the pre-union situation if no supernational fiscal authority is created. There are three types of policy actions: a) pure monetary policy, which leaves public expenditure and taxation unaltered; b) pure fiscal policy, which leaves the supply of money unaltered; c) the policy mix. In a monetary union, monetary policy must be assigned to the union central bank. As for the other instruments there are two possibilities: if fiscal policy is assigned both to the union and to the single countries, then the union will have a), b) and c) and the members b); if fiscal policy is not conducted at a supernational level, and therefore c) is not either, the union will have a) and the member countries b) only.

It seems, therefore, that although fiscal policy should not be transferred entirely to the Community, some degree of centralization could be beneficial. Chapter V will show how these conclusions differ in the case of a "big" union.

Bibliography

Campa, G. (1989): "Il ruolo della politica di bilancio nell'integrazione dell'Europa", in: *Moneta e Credito,* Nr. 167, p. 339-363.

Canzoneri, M. B.; Henderson, D. W. (1988): "Is Sovereign Policy Making Bad?", in Brunner, Karl; Meltzer, Allan H. (eds.), *Stabilization Policy and Labour Markets*, Carnegie-Rochester Conference Series on Public Policy, 28.

Cesarano, F. (1987): "La teoria delle unioni monetarie e il coordinamento delle politiche fiscali", in: *Note Economiche*, Vol.1, p. 18-30.

Corden, W. M. (1987): "On Trasmission and Coordination under Flexible Exchange Rates", in: Buiter, W.; Marston, R., *International Economic Policy Coordination*, p. 1-24.

De Grauwe, P. (1990): "Fiscal policy in the EMS: A Strategic Analysis", in: E.-M. Claasen, *International and European Monetary Systems*, Oxford 1990, p. 121-140.

Eichengreen, B. (1991): "European Monetary Unification and the Regional Unemployment Problem", *IBER Working Paper* Nr. 91-181, Berkley.

Fratianni, M.; von Hagen, J. (1990a): "The European Monetary System Ten Years After", in: *Carnegie-Rochester Conference Series on Public Policy*, Vol. 32, p. 173-242.

Fratianni, M.; von Hagen, J. (1990b): "Public Choice Aspects of European Monetary Unification", *Indiana CGB Paper*, Nr. 33.

Hamada, K. (1974): "Alternative Exchange Rate Systems and the Interdependence of Monetary Policy", in: Aliber, R. Z. (ed.), *National Monetary Policies and the International Finance System*, Chicago.

Hamada, K. (1976): "Macroeconomic Strategy and Coordination under Alternative Exchange Rates", in: Dornbusch, R.; Frenkel, J. (eds.), *International Economic Policy: Theory and Evidence*, p. 292-324.

Levin, J. H. (1983): "A model of Stabilization Policy in a Jointly Floating Currency Area", in: Bhandari, J. S.; Putnam, B. H. (eds), *Economic Interdependence and Flexible Exchange Rates*, Cambridge (Mass.), London, p. 329-349.

Niehans, J.(1968): "Monetary and Fiscal Policies in Open Economies under Fixed Exchange Rates: An Optimizing Approach", in: *Journal of Political Economy*, Vol. 76, Nr. 4, Pt. 2, p. 893-943.

Paladini, R. (1993): "L'imposizione diretta nel processo di unificazione europea", in: S. Micossi; Visco, I. (eds.), *Inflazione Concorrenza e Sviluppo: L'Economia italiana e la sfida dell'integrazione europea*, Bologna.

Siebke, J. (1992): *Implikationen modelltheoretischer Ansätze für die Harmonisierung der Fiskalpolitik in der europäischen Währungsunion*, unpublished manuscript.

Vaubel, R. (1978): *Strategies for Currency Unification*, Tübingen, p. 39-42.

Willms, M. (1990): "Der Delors-Plan und die Anforderungen an eine gemeinsame Geldpolitik", in: *Kredit und Kapital*, 23 1990 1, p. 30-59.

CHAPTER IV
AN IS-LM-AS MODEL FOR A "BIG" EXCHANGE RATE UNION

Introduction

Up to now it has been assumed that the monetary union was not "big" enough, in economic terms, to affect world economic variables, therefore considered exogenous. Abandoning this assumption involves taking into account the effects of the union policy operations on the rest of the world and their repercussions on the union itself. This requires the use of a three-component model in the real sense of the word, i. e. a model in which the relevant variables of all countries are endogenous. Examples of this type are to be found in Gries (1989) and Herberg (1991) in the context of international trade, Canzoneri/Henderson (1991) in that of international policy coordination and Wohltmann (1994) in that of exchange rate union dynamic modelling. This new system of interdependence can be given a visual representation, illustrated by Fig. I. Union member-country 1's economic changes affect both union member-country 2 and the rest of the world. The same is true for the other two components.

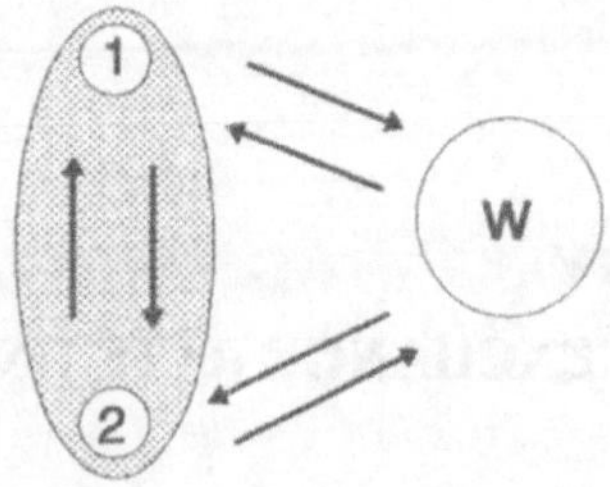

Fig. I

The interdependence system between the big union and the rest of the world.

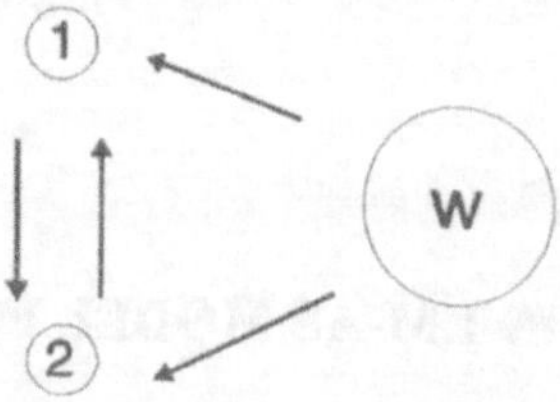

Fig.II

The interdependence system between the small union and the rest of the world.

In the case of a "small" union, instead, the direction of economic changes between the union member-countries and the rest of the world only goes in the way from the latter to the former, as illustrated in Fig. II. In the following analysis, symmetry assumptions between the union member-countries will be introduced to simplify computation: as a consequence of this, the union will act as a single block, as indicated by the shade area in Fig. I. This implies that the final results of the analysis will be, under many respects, the same as in the two-country Mundell-Fleming model (see chapter 1 for the corresponding literature; see also McKibbin/Sachs (1991) and Jarchow (1992)).

Two aspects must be kept in mind when analysing the case of a "big" union. First, the magnitude of the repercussion effects of the union policy operations will depend mainly on two factors: the efficacy on the union member-countries, the larger being this, the stronger resulting the effects on the rest of the world and their feed-back onto the union; and the relative size of the rest of the world with respect to the union, the greater being this, the smaller the influence on it of the union economic changes and the repercussions on the member countries. These elements are present in Salvatore (1992), a study with simulations of the McKibbin/Sachs Global Model analysing the real and monetary effects of the Europe 1992 program on the European Community and the United States. The results show that the EC 92 program will lead to a 6% higher GDP, 4% lower prices and a 5% real depreciation of the ECU for Europe by the year 2.000, while the effects on the USA are similar but rather smaller, the reason for the latter result being that the economic effects of the EC 92 program on the Community itself are not large and the US are still the larger economic unit in the world.

Second, in addition to the costs and benefits deriving from the completion of the unification process of the type analysed in chapter I, there are also "international" costs and benefits, deriving from the developments in the non-member countries and international institutions and their reactions to the process itself. These issues have been analysed in Alogoskoufis/Portes (1991) for the European case. They distinguish between institutional and analytical factors. The former derive from the adaptation of the G7 summits and the IMF to the presence of a European unique entity: the increased international weight of the member countries as a whole would have a counterpart in the costs deriving from the internal bargaining, necessary, for instance, to select the Minister representing the Community. The latter factors concern the international role of the ECU and the international coordination of economic policies. As for the first aspect, the completion of the EMU would reduce the intervention in dollars by the member countries, but it is still unprobable that it will replace the US currency as international means of payments, given the role played by hysteresis in this field. As for the second aspect, the presence of a second big player, the first being the USA, in the international (monetary) policy coordination game might increase for both the incentives to use the exchange rate as a policy instruments, i. e. beggar-thy-neighbour policies, with the return to an international system of flexible exchange rates. This view is shared by Goodhart (1992), who points out that the dedication of the European System of Central Banks to price stability would reduce the degree of flexibility for monetary and fiscal policy coordination.

1. The model and its formal representation

In the case of a "big" union, the assumption that world variables are exogenously fixed must be relaxed: economic changes originating in the currency area are strong enough to affect the world demand for its exports, and therefore the world income and price levels. Also the world interest rate will then be determined by the system of interdependence between the union member-countries and between these and the rest of the world. Such a system can be formally represented adapting chapter II's model in order to take into account the endogenous presence of the third component, i. e. by adding the IS, LM and AS curves for the rest of the world (equations (3), (5) and (8)). The model then becomes:

$$(1) \qquad Y_1 = C_1(\overset{+}{Y_1}, \overset{-}{r}) + G_1 + B_1(\overset{-}{Y_1}, \overset{+}{Y_2}, \overset{+}{Y_w}, \overset{+}{P_2/P_1}, \overset{+}{EP_w/P_1})$$

$$(2) \qquad Y_2 = C_2(\overset{+}{Y_2}, \overset{-}{r}) + G_2 + B_2(\overset{+}{Y_1}, \overset{-}{Y_2}, \overset{+}{Y_w}, \overset{+}{P_1/P_2}, \overset{+}{EP_w/P_2})$$

$$(3) \qquad Y_w = C_w(\overset{+}{Y_w}, \overset{-}{r}) + G_w + B_w(\overset{+}{Y_1}, \overset{+}{Y_2}, \overset{-}{Y_w}, \overset{+}{P_1/EP_w}, \overset{+}{P_2/EP_w})$$

$$(4) \qquad M_u = Q_1L_1(\overset{+}{Y_1}, \overset{-}{r}) + Q_2L_2(\overset{+}{Y_2}, \overset{-}{r})$$

$$(5) \qquad M_w = Q_wL_w(\overset{+}{Y_w}, \overset{-}{r})$$

$$(6) \qquad Y_1 = Y^s{}_1(\overset{-}{P_2/P_1}, \overset{-}{EP_w/P_1})$$

$$(7) \qquad Y_2 = Y^s{}_2(\overset{-}{P_1/P_2}, \overset{-}{EP_w/P_2})$$

$$(8) \qquad Y_w = Y^s_w(\overset{-}{P_1/EP_w}, \overset{-}{P_2/EP_w})$$

where subscripts 1, 2, u and w indicate country 1, 2, union and rest of the world economic variables respectively and, for i = 1, 2, u, w:

B_i = net exports;
C_i = private expenditure on consumption and investment goods;
E = exchange rate between the union and the rest of the world;
G_i = government expenditure;
L_i = demand for money;
M_i = supply of money;
P_i = domestic price level;
Q_i = consumer price index;
r = world interest rate;
Y_i = level of output;

and the signs above the arguments of the functions indicate the sign of the corresponding partial derivatives.

As in chapter II, the intra-union exchange rate is normalized to unity. Full capital mobility is assumed and therefore the interest rate r is the same in all countries. The union money supply, M_u, is given by the sum of the union member-countries central banks' holdings of domestic securities and total international reserves ($M_1 + M_2 + R$). The endogenous variables of the system are: Y_1, Y_2, Y_w, P_1, P_2, P_w, E, r.

An eight equation model produces long and complicated determinants, the signs and economic meanings of which cannot be specified. In order to analyse the effects of policy operations, therefore, several simplifications will be introduced; some of them are the same as in chapter II, others will consist in symmetry assumptions between the countries, as illustrated in the next section.

2. Symmetry assumptions and other simplifications introduced for computational reasons

In order to simplify the computation and make it possible to interpret the relevent multipliers, it will first be assumed that money demand does not depend on the consumer price index, but on the price of domestic output. The cost of such a simplification is the loss of real balance effects in the short run. Second, the mathematical analysis will be limited to the demand side, i. e. the short-run case, under the assumption that $P_1 = P_2 = P_w$, all being constant and normalized to unity. The supply-side reactions will be analysed only graphically, along the guideline offered by chapter II.

The short-run model would then be the following:

(1') $$Y_1 = C_1 (Y_1, r) + G_1 + B_1 (Y_1, Y_2, Y_w, E)$$

(2') $$Y_2 = C_2 (Y_2, r) + G_2 + B_2 (Y_1, Y_2, Y_w, E)$$

(3') $$Y_w = C_w (Y_w, r) + G_w + B_w (Y_1, Y_2, Y_w, E)$$

(4') $$M_u = L_1 (Y_1, r) + L_2 (Y_2, r)$$

(5') $$M_w = L_w (Y_w, r).$$

The endogenous variables of the system become five: Y_1, Y_2, Y_w, E, r. Finally, the two union member-countries will be considered to have symmetric reactions to changes in the endogenous variables. This will allow for the use of the method developed in Aoki (1981), which has been used in the recent literature on exchange rate unions in the context of three-country models with exogenous rest of the world variables, e. g. Feuerstein/Siebke (1990) and Wohltmann (1993). This method will however be used only in sections 6 and 10, when the case of fixed exchange rates between the union and the rest of the world will be analysed with the help of a further symmetry assumption, that between the union as a whole and the rest of the world. In the case of flexible exchange rates, instead, this assumption is neither necessary nor easily applicable, at least without introducing further limitations, given the built-in asymmetry between the intra-union fixed exchange rate and the flexible one with the rest of the world, together with the endogeneity of the interest rate. Moreover, it is throughout assumed that the union as a whole and the rest of the world react symmetrically, and not that each union member-country has the same reactions to changes in the endogenous variables as the other member and the rest of the world, which also prevents from directly applying the method developed by Aoki for the three-country case.

If one assumes that country 1 and country 2 react symmetrically to changes in the endogenous variables and that at the initial point these take the same value in both union members, then one can add equations (1') and (2'), letting the system determine $(Y_1 + Y_2)$, i. e. the union income level, instead of Y_1 and Y_2 separately. Making this operation and differentiating one gets:

$$(1^*)\ dY_1+dY_2 = C_{uYu}(dY_1+dY_2)+2C_{ur}dr+(dG_1+dG_2)+T_{uYu}(dY_1+dY_2) +2T_{uYw}dY_w+2T_{uE}dE$$

$$(2^*)\ dY_w = C_{wYw}dY_w + C_{wr}dr + dG_w - 2T_{uYu}(dY_1 + dY_2) - 2T_{uYw}dY_w - 2\ T_EdE$$

$$(3^*)\ dM_u = L_{uYu}\ (dY_1 + dY_2) + 2\ L_{ur}\ dr$$

$$(4^*)\ dM_w = L_{wYw}\ dY_w + L_{wr}\ dr$$

where:

T_i = net exports;

and:

$$C_{1Y1} = C_{2Y2} = C_{uYu}$$
$$C_{1r} = C_{2r} = C_{ur}$$
$$L_{1Y1} = L_{2Y2} = L_{uYu}$$
$$L_{1r} = L_{2r} = L_{ur}$$
$$T_{1Y1} = T_{1Y2} = T_{uYu}.$$

Note that the union net exports are the opposite of the rest of the world ones, i. e.:

$$T_w = - T_u.$$

This model will be now used to analyse the effects on the endogenous variables of the system, $(Y_1 + Y_2)$, Y_w, E and r of monetary and fiscal policy operations occuring in the union and in the rest of the world.

3. The efficacy of monetary policy: the short run

The effects of an increase in the union money stock will now be considered. One can speak of a union money supply since, as shown in chapter II, with fixed exchange rates and perfect capital mobility the money stock and the money market are unique for the entire currency area. An increase in M_u causes the union interest rate to go down: the union income level, $(Y_1 + Y_2)$, rises through the expansionary effects on consumption and investment, $(C_1 + C_2)$. The decrease in the interest rate produces a further expansionary effect through the depreciation of the exchange rate, in response to the incipient massive capital outflow from the union member-countries towards the rest of the world: the union trade balance improves, while the opposite is true for the rest of the world, where the appreciation causes a decrease in income, so that eventually the world interest rate remains at a level lower than the initial one. The results obtained are the same as in a two-country world (union and rest of the world) with flexible exchange rates, since the introduction of the symmetry assumption makes the union behave as a single block.

These results can be shown graphically, as illustrated in Fig. 1(a) for the union and 1(b) for the rest of the world. The initial equilibrium position is denoted by point *A*. The increase in M_u causes the LM curve of the union to shift to the right to LM'. At the new intersection point with the IS curve, *B*, the interest rate would be below the rest of the world one, so that the exchange rate depreciates in response to the incipient massive capital outflow (and appreciates from the rest of the world point of view in response to the incipient massive capital inflow): the IS curve of the union shifts to the right to IS' because of the increase in competitiveness, with income and the interest rate both increasing, while the IS curve of the rest of the world shifts to the left, with income and the interest rate both going down. The final position is denoted by point *C*: the effect on the union income level is expansionary, that on the rest of the world contractionary; the interest rate is lower than before the monetary expansion.

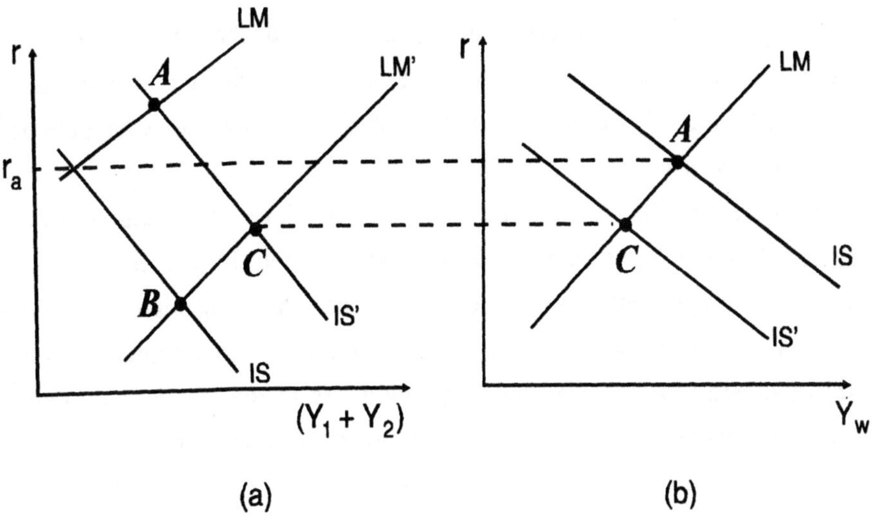

Fig. 1: A monetary expansion is a "beggar-thy-neighbour" type of policy in the short run under flexible exchange rates.

This analysis is confirmed by the signs and values of the multipliers derived from the system of equations (1*) - (4*):

$$(dY_1 + dY_2)/dM_u = -2T_{uE}[(1-C_{wYw})L_{wr}+L_{wYw}(C_{wr}+C_{ur})]/|D| > 0$$

$$dY_w/dM_u = + 2\, T_{uE}\, [L_{wr}\, (1-C_{uYu})]/|D| < 0$$

$$dr/dM_u = - 2\, T_{uE}\, [L_{wYw}\, (1-C_{uYu})]/|D| < 0$$

$$dE/dM_u=-\{(1-C_{uYu}-T_{uYu})[(1-C_{wYw}+2T_{uYw})L_{wr}+C_{wr}L_{wYw}]-T_{uYu}(2C_{ur}L_{wYw}-2T_{uYw}L_{wr})\}/|D| > 0$$

where:

$$|D| = 2T_{uE}\{-L_{wYw}2L_{ur}(1-C_{uYu})-L_{uYu}L_{wr}(1-C_{wYw})-L_{uYu}L_{wYw}(C_{wr}+2C_{ur})\} > 0.$$

What do these results say, also in comparison with those obtained in chapter II? As for the effect on the union member-counties income levels, monetary policy is expansionary; given the symmetry assumption, the magnitude is the same in both member countries. Such a result resembles that of chapter II both in the sign and in the process leading to it: the mechanism, actually, works through the responsiveness of the trade balance to changes in the exchange rate, as the term T_{uE} appearing in the multipliers shows, as it happens in the "small" union case.

The effect on the rest of the world income level is of course absent in chapter II, where Y_w is considered exogenously fixed. In this case, a monetary expansion has a contractionary effect abroad, the transmission mechanism being again the responsiveness of the trade balance to the appreciation of the exchange rate towards the monetary union. As in the standard two-country flexible exchange rate case, therefore, a monetary expansion is a "beggar-thy-neighbour" type of policy operation. Another "new" effect is that on the now endogenous interest rate: an expansionary monetary policy in the "big" union decreases the world interest rate and the transmission mechanism is the same as for income: r does not go back to the original level because of the fall in Y_w due to the increase in E. Finally, the effect on the exchange rate between the union currency (-ies) and that of the rest of the world is a depreciation, due to the downward pressure exerted on the interest rate by the monetary expansion.

In the case of a monetary expansion in the rest of the world, the reverse of the above results is obtained; the multipliers are reported here for the sake of completeness:

$$(dY_1 + dY_2)/dM_w = +2\, T_{uE}\,[2\, L_{ur}\,(1-C_{wYw})]/|D| < 0$$

$$dY_w/dM_w = -2T_{uE}[(1-C_{uYu})2L_{ur}+L_{uYu}(C_{wr}+2C_{ur})]/|D| > 0$$

$$dr/dM_w = +2\,T_{uE}\,[-L_{uYu}\,(1-C_{wYw})]/|D| < 0$$

$$dE/dM_w=\{(1-C_{wYw}-2T_{uYw})[(1-C_{uYu}-T_{uYu})2L_{ur}+2C_{ur}L_{uYu}]+2T_{uYw}(C_{wr}L_{uYu}+T_{uYu}2L_{ur})\}/|D| < 0.$$

4. The efficacy of monetary policy: the medium run

In the medium term, prices cannot be considered fixed: supply side reactions to changes in aggregate demand must be taken into account, in the sense that producers are not willing to supply any amount of output demanded at the given price level, but that there exists a positive relationship between the amount of output supplied and its price. Therefore, equations (1') - (3') must be replaced by equations (1) - (3), equations (4') and (5') by equations (4) and (5), with P_1 instead of Q_1 and P_2 instead of Q_2 if one does not consider real balance effects in the short run. As for the supply functions, assuming that in the medium-run wages do not have time to adjust to the change in prices, equations (6) - (8) become:

(6') $$Y^s_1 = Y^s_1\,(P_1)$$

(7') $$Y^s_2 = Y^s_2\,(P_2)$$

(8') $$Y^s_w = Y^s_w\,(P_w).$$

Even introducing the symmetry assumptions for the two union member-countries, i. e. pooling together equations (1) and (2) on the demand side and (6') and (7') on the supply one, one is still left with a six-equation system, which produces determinants very complex to calculate and multipliers too difficult to be interpreted. Therefore, the analysis will be limited to the graphical one. The results are nevertheless undubious, with no need for a quantitative counterproof, also because of the help of the guideline given by chapter II's outcomes.

The price effect works, as far as the demand side is concerned, through two channels: the trade balance, which improves (worsens) if the relative price of domestic output decreases (increases), and real money balances, which increase (decrease) inversely with respect to price changes. Graphically, these effects translate themselves into shifts of the IS and LM curves. Given equations (6') - (8'), in the (Y, P) space, one has a positively sloped AS curve.

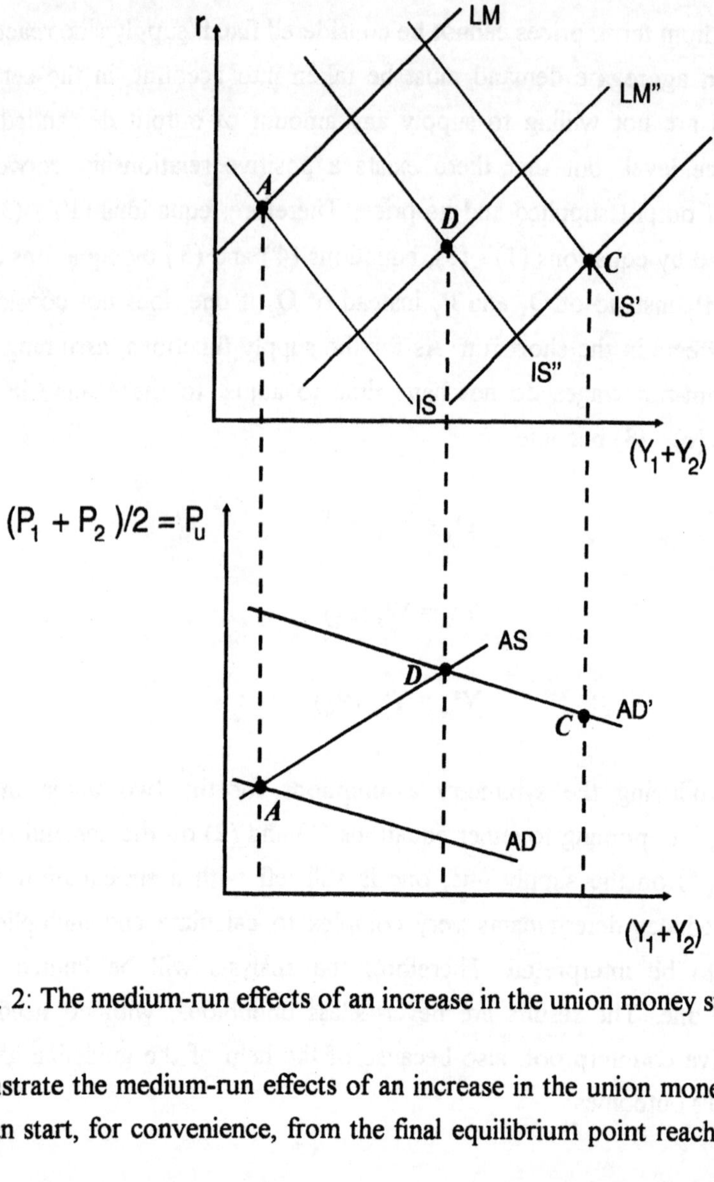

Fig. 2: The medium-run effects of an increase in the union money supply.

To illustrate the medium-run effects of an increase in the union money supply one can start, for convenience, from the final equilibrium point reached in the short-run span, i. e point *C* of Fig. 1, since the previous analysis still applies. Fig. 2 refers to the union as a whole, Fig. 3 to the rest of the world. The rightward shift of the union IS and LM curves which brings the equilibrium point from *A* to *C* has its counterpart, in the (Y, P) diagram, in the rightward shift of the AD curve. Assuming fixed prices, i. e. an aggregate supply curve with infinite elasticity, the new equilibrium point would be *C*, with increased income and unchanged prices. If, however, the AD curve is moving along a positively sloped AS curve, the same outward shift will lead to the equilibrium point indicated by *D*, with a smaller increase in income and an increase in the price level from P_A to P_D. In the (Y, r) diagram, the increase in prices is represented by the backward shift of the IS' and LM' to IS" and LM" respectively. The new equilibrium level of the interest rate, r_D, is now higher than before.

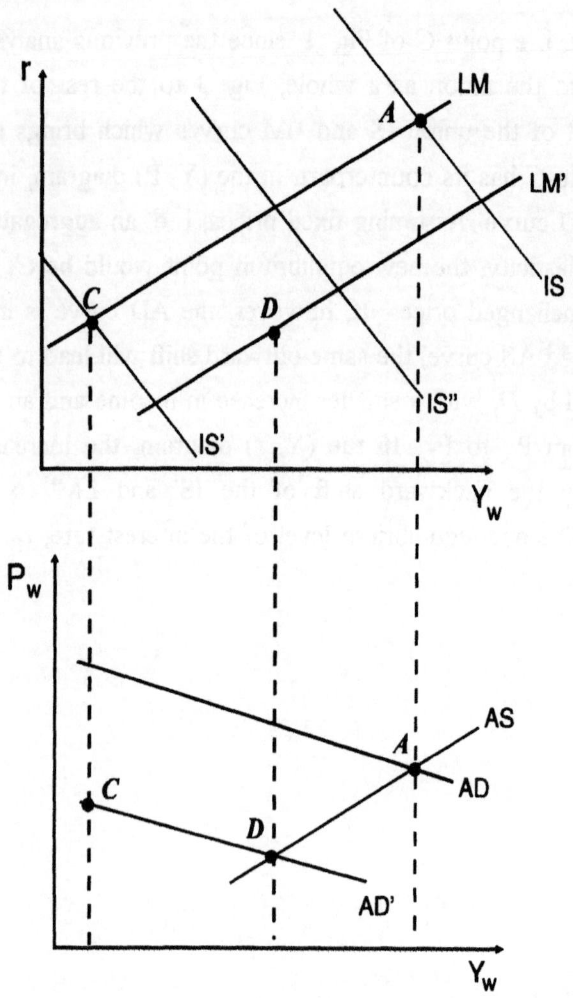

Fig. 3: The medium-run effects on the rest of the world of an increase in the union money supply.

As for the rest of the world, the backward shift of the IS curve to IS', leading to the equilibrium point C, corresponds, in the (Y, P) diagram, to the leftward shift of the AD curve, measured by the segment AC. Once again, if this shift occurs along a positively sloped AS curve, the final position corresponds to a smaller decrease of the income level and a decrease of the price level. The latter outcome is represented, in the (Y, r) diagram, by a rightward shift of the IS and LM curves to IS" and LM' respectively.

To conclude, the qualitative results obtained are the same as before: monetary policy is expansionary at home and contractionary abroad; the world

world interest rate decreases and the union exchange rate depreciates. However, magnitudes differ: the rise of the price level in the union, consequent to the increase in aggregate demand, counteracts the expansionary effect of the policy operation, while the reverse is true for the rest of the world, where the contractionary effect is mitigated by the fall in the price level.

5. The efficacy of monetary policy: the long run

In the long run wages have time to adjust to changes in the consumer price level: these do not derive only from changes in the price of domestic output, but also of the imported goods, i.e. changes in foreign prices and the exchange rate. If workers take their decisions on the amount of labour to supply with regard to the level of their "consumption wage", then an appreciation (depreciation) of the exchange rate makes foreign goods cheaper (more expensive) and increases (decreases) the purchasing power of the domestic wage, thus leading to an increase (decrease) of the supply of labour for a given level of the nominal wage. Therefore, the supply of goods is dependent on the real exchange rate towards the rest of the world, which is a shift variable of the aggregate supply curve, in its (Y, P) space representation. Equations (6') - (8') should then be replaced by equations (6) - (8). Once again, even introducing the symmetry assumption for the union member-countries, reducing the number of equations from eight to six and letting therefore the system determine the union income and price levels instead of those of the single member countries, one is left with multipliers which are too complex to be given a sign and an economic interpretation. Therefore, the mathematical analysis will be skipped, also because the qualitative results can clearly be obtained on the basis of chapter II's conceptual and mathematical outcomes. Suffice to say that the union aggregate supply function is now a positive function of the term of trade, t, defined as the reciprocal of the real exchange rate, while the opposite is true for the rest of the world aggregate supply function, i. e.:

$$\text{(6'')} \qquad Y_1 + Y_2 = f(\overset{+}{t})$$

$$\text{(8'')} \qquad Y_w = f(t).$$

In order to illustrate the long-run effects of an increase in the union money supply, it is again convenient to start from the medium-run final position, i. e. point *D* of Figs. 2 and 3, reproduced in Figs. 4, referring to the union, and 5, representing the rest of the world, since the previous analysis still applies.

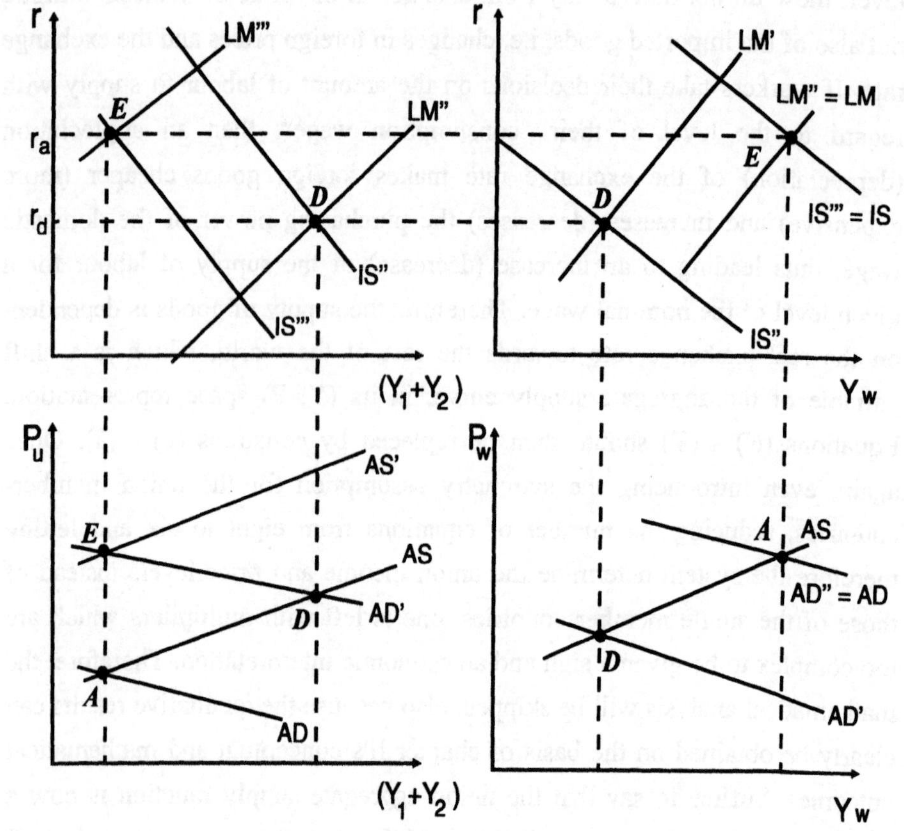

Fig. 4 Fig. 5

The ineffectiveness of monetary policy in the long-run.

At point *D* in Fig. 4, given the depreciation of E, the consumption wage of the union workers has decreased: labour supply is reduced, for a given nominal wage level, and the AS curve shifts to the left. The consequent increase in prices makes also the union IS and LM curves shift backwards. On the basis of chapter II's findings, one can say that this process ends once point *E* has been reached, with income and the interest rate back to the original levels, but higher prices.

As for the rest of the world, the increase in P_w makes the IS" and AD shift back to their original positions, while the AS curve does not shift because, in the end, E and P_u have increased proportionally and therefore there is no change in the consumer price index and in wages. At the end of the process, income and the price level have gone back to their initial levels. The results resemble those of chapter II for the "small" union case: monetary policy has no effect on income in the long run, either at home or abroad; what changes is the home price level, which increases.

6. The efficacy of monetary policy: the case of fixed exchange rates between the union and the rest of the world

In this paragraph the "big" union model is applied to the case of fixed exchange rates with the rest of the world. This can be useful for two reasons: first, the comparison with the flexible exchange rate case can help in understanding the effects of the change from a system of internationally fixed exchange rates to a flexible exchange rate regime; second, if the union is big enough to affect the rest of the world economic variables, but still relatively small with respect to it, it might choose to renounce the exchange rate as a policy instrument, i. e. beggar-thy-neighbour policies, opting for a fixed exchange rate regime. Thomsen (1992) analyses the case of a "small" exchange rate union having fixed exchange rates with the rest of the world and this study will be referred to in comparing the results obtained for the "big" union case.

The mathematical analysis will again be limited to the short-run case. With some minor adaptation with respect to the preceding sections, the model is then the following (R_i = international reserves; U_1 = trade balance of country 1 towards country 2; rest of notations as usual):

(1") $Y_1 = C_1(Y_1, r) + G_1 + U_1(Y_1, Y_2) + T_1(Y_1, Y_w, E)$

(2") $Y_2 = C_2(Y_2, r) + G_2 - U_1(Y_1, Y_2) + T_2(Y_2, Y_w, E)$

(3") $Y_w = C_w(Y_w, r) + G_w - T_1(Y_1, Y_w, E) - T_2(Y_2, Y_w, E)$

(4") $M_u + R_u = L_1(Y_1, r) + L_2(Y_2, r)$

(5") $M_w + R_w = L_w(Y_w, r)$.

Being $dR_u = - dR_w = dR$, the system has five endogenous variables: Y_1, Y_2, Y_w, r, R. Two ways of simplifying this system, in order to make calculation easier and the results interpretable, will now be developed.

I) A unique world money supply and symmetry between the two union member-countries

The first way consists in the two following steps.

1) With perfect international capital mobility and fixed exchange rates, the critical variable, as far as monetary policy is concerned, is the world money supply. In fact, the national money stocks are not exogenous any more, since private assets holders have access to the world capital market; moreover, the effect of monetary operations is independent of the country where they are undertaken. Therefore, one can add equations (4") and (5"), thus obtaining a unique money market equilibrium equation:

(6") $M = L_1(Y_1, r) + L_2(Y_2, r) + EL_w(Y_w, r)$,

where:

$$M = M_u + EM_w$$

(reserves cancel out).

2) The second step consists in introducing the symmetry assumption for the two union member-countries' reactions to changes in the endogenous variables and adding equations (1") and (2"), as it had been done in section 2. Then, taking the total differential, one gets:

$$(1°)\quad (1\text{-}C_{uYu}\text{-}T_{uYu})(dY_1+dY_2)\text{-}2T_{uYw}dY_w\text{-}2C_{ur}dr = (dG_1+dG_2)+2T_{uE}dE$$

$$(2°)\quad T_{uYu}(dY_1+dY_2)+(1\text{-}C_{wYw}+2T_{uYw})dY_w\text{-}C_{wr}dr=dG_w\text{-}2T_{uE}dE$$

$$(3°)\quad L_{uYu}(dY_1+dY_2)+EL_{wYw}dY_w+(2L_{ur}+EL_{wr})dr=dM\text{-}L_w(Y_w,r)dE.$$

The endogenous variables are (Y_1+Y_2), Y_w and r. The effects of an increase in the world money supply will now be analysed. As specified above, these are the same whatever country the monetary disturbance comes from. The monetary policy multipliers are:

$$(dY_1+dY_2)/dM = [2T_{uYw}C_{wr}+2C_{ur}(1\text{-}C_{wYw}+2T_{uYw})]/|D_1| > 0$$

$$dY_w/dM = [C_{wr}(1\text{-}C_{uYu}\text{-}T_{uYu})\text{-}2C_{ur}T_{uYu}]/|D_1| > 0$$

$$dr/dM = [(1\text{-}C_{uYu}\text{-}T_{uYu})(1\text{-}C_{wYw}+2T_{uYw})+2T_{uYw}T_{uYu}]/|D_1| < 0$$

where:

$$|D_1|=(1\text{-}C_{uYu}\text{-}T_{uYu})[(1\text{-}C_{wYw}+2T_{uYw})(2L_{ur}+EL_{wr})C_{wr}EL_{wYw}]\text{-}T_{uYu}[\text{-}2T_{uYw}(2L_{ur}+EL_{wr})+ 2C_{ur}EL_{wYw}]+L_{uYu}[2T_{uYw}C_{wr}+2C_{ur}(1\text{-}C_{wYw}+2T_{uYw})] < 0.$$

These results show that an increase in the money supply, e. g. through an expansionary operation undertaken by the union monetary authorities, causes an increase in both the union and the rest of the world income levels through a decrease of the world interest rate. This happens because the increase in the money supply is redistributed between country 1, country 2 and the rest of the world according to the tastes of the private asset holders and consequently through the change in reserves necessary to keep the exchange rate fixed. The decrease in the interest rate level, which boosts demand, is therefore present both in the union and in the rest of the world.

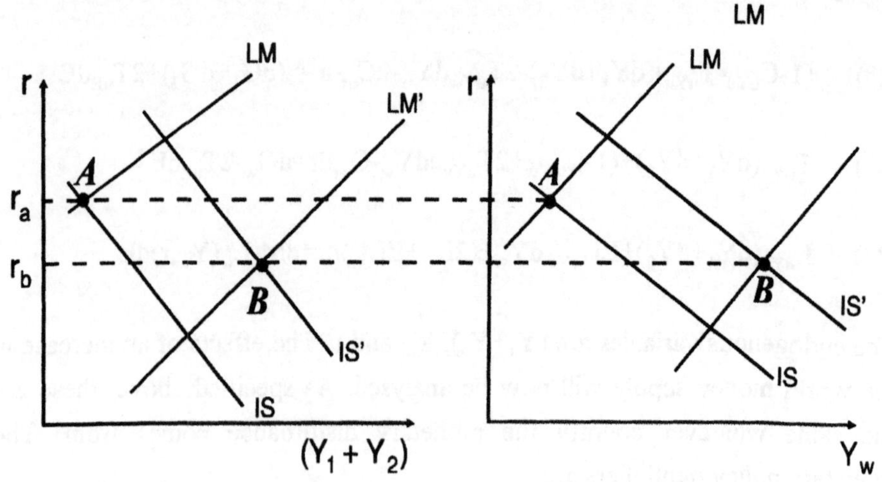

Fig. 6: The positive transmission of monetary policy under fixed exchange rates.

Graphically (see Fig. 6), the increase in M causes a rightward shift of both the union and the rest of the world LM curves to LM', so that the interest rate decreases. A further adjustment process comes through the rightward shift of the IS curves induced by the trade linkage effect, until a new equilibrium point, such as *B*, is reached, with a lower world interest rate and higher income levels for all countries. As for the distribution of the increase in income between the two union member-countries, because of the symmetry assumption and the fixed exchange rate regime existing between them, they will experience an equal increase in income.

As far as the medium run is concerned, the usual conclusion applies, i. e. the multipliers have the same sign as in the short run but smaller magnitudes because of the price effect which counteracts the initial expansion.

II) Symmetry between the union member-countries and between the union and the rest of the world

The other way to simplify the model consists in introducing not only the assumption that the union member-countries react symmetrically to changes in the endogenous variables, but also that the same is true for the union as a whole and the rest of the world, i. e.:

$$C_{wYw} = C_{uYu};$$
$$C_{wr} = 2C_{ur};$$
$$L_{wYw} = L_{uYu};$$
$$L_{wr} = 2L_{ur}.$$

This allows to use the Aoki's method, which consists in subdividing the system into two independent subsystems, one describing the effects of changes in the exogenous variables on the union and the rest of the world as a whole, the other the difference between the induced changes in the union and rest of the world variables. Therefore, given that $dR_w = - dR_u = - dR$ and normalizing E, the fixed exchange rate between the union and the rest of the world to unity, one obtains:

a) Subsystem "sum":

(1s) $$(1-C_{uYu})[dY_w+(dY_1+dY_2)]-4C_{ur}dr = (dG_1+dG_2)+dG_w$$

(2s) $$L_{uYu}[(dY_1+dY_2)+dY_w]+4L_{ur}dr = dM_u+dM_w$$

where equation (1s) is derived from the sum of equations [(1") + (2")] and (3"), while equation (2s) from that of equations (4") and (5"), given the symmetry assumption. This subsystem determines $[(dY_1+dY_2)+dY_w]$ and dr.

b) Subsystem difference:

(1d) $$(1-C_{uYu}+2T_{uYu})[dY_w-(dY_1+dY_2)] = dG_w-(dG_1+dG_2)$$

(2d) $$2dR+L_{uYu}[dY_w-(dY_1+dY_2)] = dM_w-dM_u$$

where equation (1d) is derived from the difference between equation (3") and the sum of equations (1") and (2"), while (2d) is the difference between equation (4") and (5"). This subsystem determines $[dY_w-(dY_1+dY_2)]$ and dR.

As for the effects of a monetary policy operation, the first subsystem yields:

$$[dY_w+(dY_1+dY_2)]/(dM_w+dM_u) = 4C_{ur}/|D_2| > 0$$

$$dr/(dM_w+dM_u) = (1-C_{uYu})/|D_2| < 0$$

where:

$$|D_2| = (1-C_{uYu})4L_{ur}+4C_{ur}L_{uYu} < 0.$$

The second subsystem yields:

$$[dY_w-(dY_1+dY_2)]/(dM_w-dM_u) = 0$$

$$dR/(dM_w-dM_u) = (1-C_{uYu}+2T_{uYu})/|D_3| > 0 = ½$$

where:

$$|D_3| = 2(1-C_{uYu}+2T_{uYu}) > 0.$$

To obtain the effect on dY_w and (dY_1+dY_2) separately, note that:

$$dY_w = \{[dY_w+(dY_1+dY_2)]+[dY_w-(dY_1+dY_2)]\}/2$$

$$(dY_1+dY_2) = \{[dY_w+(dY_1+dY_2)]-[dY_w-(dY_1+dY_2)]\}/2.$$

Therefore:

$$(dY_1+dY_2)/dM_u=(dY_1+dY_2)/dM_w= ½ \{[dY_w+(dY_1+dY_2)]/dM_u\}=2C_{ur}/|D_2| > 0$$

$$dY_w/dM_u = dY_w/dM_w = ½ \{[dY_w+(dY_1+dY_2)]/dM_u\} + 0 = 2C_{ur}/|D_2| > 0.$$

The result that monetary policy has a positive effect on the income levels of the union and the rest of the world whatever country undertook the operation is confirmed. Given the symmetry assumption between the union and the rest of the world, the effect is also quantitatively the same in both of them. The world interest rate goes down because of the monetary expansion. The effect on reserves is such that those of the country undertaking the operation decrease (by 50%), as one would have expected. With respect to the small union fixed exchange rate case, it is now no longer true that monetary policy is ineffective: this is because also the world interest rate and the rest of the world output are affected by economic changes occuring within the union, i. e. the change in its money supply is not unperceptible as far as the world money supply is concerned. In contrast with the big union flexible exchange rate case, monetary policy is not of the "beggar-thy-neighbour" type and the expansionary effect is distributed between the union and the rest of the world.

7. The efficacy of fiscal policy: the short run

The model of equations (1*) - (4*) is also useful in accounting for changes in the union and rest of world income levels induced by a fiscal expansion, undertaken, for instance, in country 1. The increase in G_1 causes an increase in $(Y_1 + Y_2)$. The new income level is compatible with a higher interest rate: this attracts capital flows, with the consequence of an appreciation of the exchange rate, which acts as a stabilizing mechanism pushing the income level down because of the worsening of the trade balance. The appreciation, however, also affects the rest of the world income level, which increases through the improved trade balance. The decrease in $(Y_1 + Y_2)$ and the increase in Y_w, moreover, tend to reduce the expansionary, for the rest of the world, and contractionary, for the union, trade balance effects induced by the appreciation of E. All these forces and their repercussions might well involve further changes in E, even of opposite sign with respect to the initial appreciation, until a new equilibrium is reached, with higher income everywhere and a higher level of the world interest rate. Once again, since the introduction of the symmetry assumption makes the union member-countries behave as a single block floating with respect to the rest of the world, the results resemble those of the two-country Mundell-Fleming model with flexible exchange rates.

The process and the results can be shown also graphically. The initial equilibrium position is denoted by point *A* in Fig. 7.

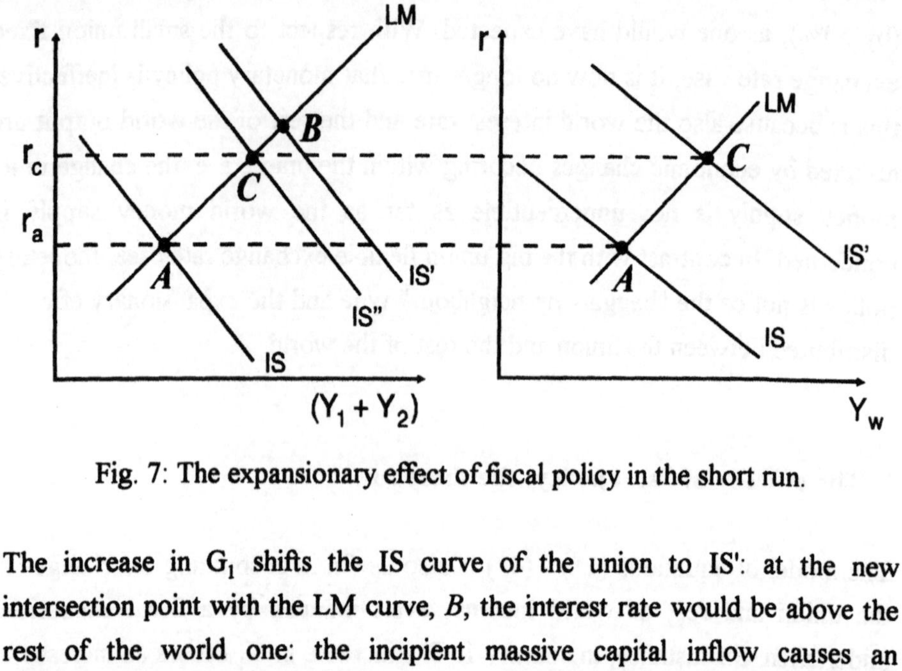

Fig. 7: The expansionary effect of fiscal policy in the short run.

The increase in G_1 shifts the IS curve of the union to IS': at the new intersection point with the LM curve, *B*, the interest rate would be above the rest of the world one: the incipient massive capital inflow causes an appreciation of the external exchange rate. This improves the rest of the world trade balance and worsens that of the union. Therefore, the IS curve of the former shifts to the right and that of the latter to the left, until a final equilibrium point such as *C* is reached, the relative difference in the income changes being determined by the relative slope of the LM curves.

Algebraically, the system yields the following fiscal policy multipliers:

$$(dY_1+dY_2)/(dG_1+dG_2) = [2T_{uE}(-2L_{ur}L_{wYw})]/|D| > 0$$

$$dY_w/(dG_1+dG_2) = -2T_{uE}L_{uYu}L_{wr}/|D| > 0$$

$$dr/(dG_1+dG_2) = 2T_{uE}L_{uYu}L_{wYw}/|D| > 0$$

$$dE/(dG_1+dG_2) = \{2T_{uYu}L_{ur}L_{wYw}+L_{uYu}[(1-C_{wYw}+2T_{uYw})L_{wr}+C_{wr}L_{wYw}]\}/|D| < 0$$
(if T_{uYu} is small)

where |D| is the same as in section 3 and dG_2 is equal to zero.

The multipliers clearly indicate in the sensitivity of the trade balance the fundamental mechanism of the process. Moreover, they show that the increase in the level of income in the rest of the world is relatively larger than that in the union, the relatively flatter the LM curve of the former in comparison with that of the latter (and viceversa) and that the effect on r will be the stronger, the higher the sensitivity of money demand to changes in income.

As for the transmission within the exchange rate union, the effect on Y_2 is of ambiguous sign. In the small union case, the increase in G_1 caused an increase in Y_1 and in Y_2 through the trade linkage mechanism; however, the upward pressure on the interest rate caused an appreciation of E, worsening the union member-countries trade balances, and equilibrium in the money market required Y_2 to decrease. Now the world interest rate is no longer exogenously fixed; instead, it rises because of the fiscal expansion in country 1. Y_2 is subject to an expansionary force coming from the trade balance with the rest of the union, since Y_1 increases, a contractionary one coming from the increase in the interest rate and, in the "normal" case, a contractionary one coming from the appreciation of E. The ambiguity of the result is not solved looking at the money market, where the supply of money of country 2 decreases because of the outflow of reserves towards country 1 and the demand for money decreases as well because of the increase in r, so that Y_2 could either decrease or increase. This result is not inconsistent with that obtained for the small union, since now both Y_w and r have increased, as already pointed out in Levin (1983).

For completeness, the multipliers of a fiscal expansion in the rest of the world are now reported:

$$(dY_1+dY_2)/dG_w = -4T_{uE}L_{ur}L_{wYw}/|D| > 0$$

$$dY_w/dG_w = -2T_{uE}L_{uYu}L_{wr}/|D| > 0$$

$$dr/dG_w = 2T_{uE}L_{uYu}L_{wYw}/|D| > 0$$

$$dE/dG_w = [-(1-C_{uYu}-T_{uYu})2L_{ur}L_{wYw}-L_{uYu}(-2T_{uYw}L_{wr}+2C_{ur}L_{wYw})]/\ |D| \gtrless 0.$$

8. The efficacy of fiscal policy: the medium run

The same conderations apply here as for the case of monetary policy, i. e. the change in the price level mitigates the effect of the fiscal operation on income. The modifications of the model and the price effects are those illustrated in section 4 and will not be repeated here. In order to illustrate the medium-run effects of an increase in country 1's government expenditure it is convenient to start from the short-run equilibrium point, i. e. point *C* in Fig. 7, since the previous analysis of the demand side still applies.

The shift of the union IS curve to IS" induced by the fiscal expenditure in country 1, shown in Fig. 8, corresponds, in the (Y, P) diagram, to the rightward shift of the AD curve, measured by the segment AC. Point *C* indicates the new equilibrium at unchanged prices. If one relaxes the assumption of fixed prices, however, the AD curve moves along a positively sloped aggregate supply curve, and the outward shift leads to the equilibrium point *D*, with a smaller increase in income due to the increase in prices from P_u^A to P_u^D. In the (Y, r) space, the price effect is shown by the backward shifts of IS" and LM to IS"' and LM' respectively. The new interest rate, r_D, is lower than in the short-run case.

As for the rest of the world, Fig. 9 shows the outward shift of the IS curve to IS', leading to the equilibrium point *C*, which corresponds, in the (Y, P) diagram, to the rightward shift of the aggregate demand curve from AD to AD', measured by the segment AC. Once again, with endogenous prices, the horizontal shift does not correspond to the increase income: with a positively sloped AS curve, the final medium-run equilibrium is shown by point *D*, which corresponds to a smaller expansion of the income level, accompanied by a price increase. In the (Y, r) diagram, the price effect is represented by the leftward shifts of IS' and LM to IS" and LM' respectively.

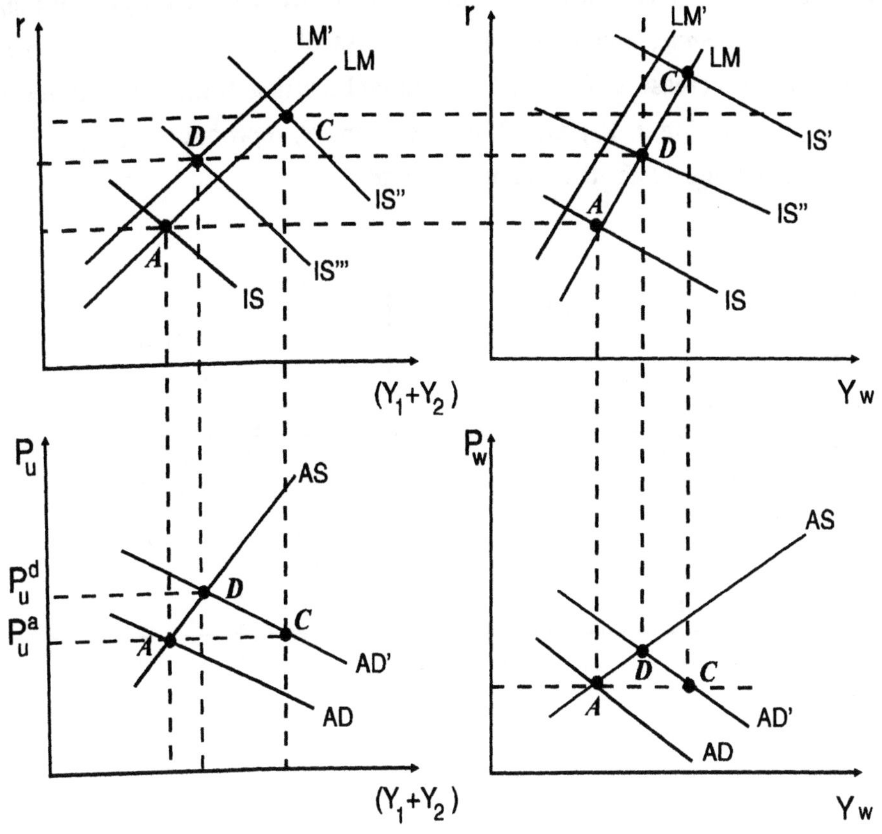

Fig. 8 Fig. 9

The medium-run efficacy of fiscal policy.

The medium-term qualitative results are the same as in the short run: fiscal policy is expansionary both at home and abroad, with the world interest rate increasing. However, magnitudes differ: the rise of the price level, consequent to the increase in aggregate demand, counteracts the expansionary effect on income of the policy operation.

9. The efficacy of fiscal policy: the long run

As described in section 5, which is to be refferred to for the model modifications adopted here, in the long run the effects of changes in the terms of trade on the position of the aggregate supply curve must be taken into account. In particular, it has been shown that an increase in the terms of trade, by increasing the purchasing power of the wage, will induce a rightward shift of the AS schedule, and viceversa in the case of a decrease. The long-run effects of an increase in G_1 will be illustrated starting from the medium-run equilibrium position, i. e. point *D* in Figs. 8 and 9, reproduced in Fig. 10 for the union and Fig. 11 for the rest of the world.

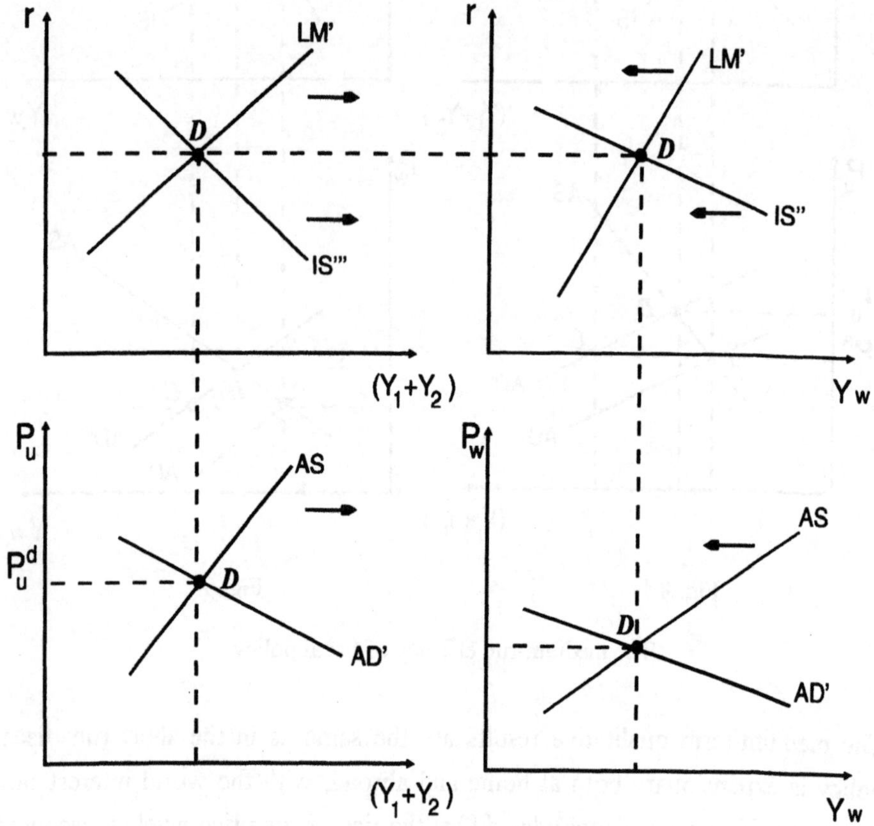

Fig. 10 Fig. 11

The long-run efficacy of fiscal policy.

The union fiscal expansion causes an increase in the terms of trade and therefore the union aggregate supply curve shifts to the right, thus strengthening the expansionary effect of the policy operation. In the (Y, r) diagram, correspondingly, IS''' and LM' would shift to the right (see arrows in Fig. 10) because of the decrease in prices. The aggregate supply of the rest of the world, instead, shifts up and to the left, the short-run expansionary effect being therefore reversed; IS'' and LM' would also shift leftwards because of the prise rise effect (see arrows in Fig. 11).

10. The efficacy of fiscal policy: the case of fixed exchange rates towards the rest of the world

As in section 6 for monetary policy, the "big" union model is here applied to the case of fixed exchange rates towards the rest of the world in order to analyse the effects of fiscal policy operations and compare them with those obtained under the assumption of a flexible exchange rate regime. The model being used is that of equations (1") - (5"), in the two simplified versions adopted in section 6.

I) A unique world money supply and symmetry between the two union member-countries

The model is that of equations (1°) - (3°), the endogenous variables of the system being $(Y_1 + Y_2)$, Y_w and r, and will be used to analyse the effects on the union and rest of the world income levels and the world interest rate induced by an increase in country 1's government expenditure. The values of the fiscal policy multipliers are:

$$(dY_1+dY_2)/dG_1 = [(1-C_{wYw}+2T_{uYw})(2L_{ur}+EL_{wr})+C_{wr}EL_{wYw}]/|D_1| > 0$$

$$dY_w/dG_1 = -\{[T_{uYu}(2L_{ur}+EL_{wr})+C_{wr}L_{uYu}]\}/|D_1| \gtrless 0$$

$$dr/dG_1 = [T_{uYu}EL_{wYw}-(1-C_{wYw}+2T_{uYw})L_{uYu}]/|D_1| > 0$$

where $|D_1|$ is as in section 6.

The effect of an increase in G_1 is therefore expansionary for the union and has an uncertain effect on the rest of the world income level, while the world interest rate rises. This is so because the increase in government expenditure boosts demand in the union (for the transmission of the expansionary effect in the union see section 7). The consequent increase in income causes an increase in the demand for money and therefore a rise in the interest rate. This would involve a capital inflow and the union monetary authorities must sell their own currency to keep the exchange rate at the fixed parity: the union money stock rises through the increase in international reserves, the interest rate must go down to re-equilibrate the excess of the supply of money over demand and therefore income rises further.

As for the rest of the world, the ambiguity of the result is due to the working of two contrasting effects: the trade linkage effect, which pushes towards an increase in income through the augmented world demand for the rest of the world output induced by the rise in the union income level; and the increase in the union interest rate, which exerts a downward pressure on E through the capital outflow: this obliges the rest of the world monetary authorities to buy their own currency loosing reserves: the fall in the money stock makes the interest rate rise, which has a contractionary effect on Y_w. These two contrasting effects can be read in the multiplier, the former (expansionary) being denoted by the term $T_{uYu}(2L_{ur}+EL_{wr})$, the latter (contractionary) by $C_{wr}L_{uYu}$.

As for the world interest rate, the effect is clearly positive, i. e. it rises with respect to the initial equilibrium position. The process can be given also a graphical representation (see Fig. 12). The increase in G_1 shifts the union IS curve rightwards to IS'. The new intersection point with the LM curve is *B* and the incipient appreciation, due to the interest rate being now above the world level, causes the intervention of the monetary authorities: foreign reserves increase and the LM curve shifts rightwards to LM', the new equilibrium point being *C*. As for the rest of the world, the increase in $(Y_1 + Y_2)$ improves the trade balance, thus causing a rightward shift of the IS curve, while the money outflow makes the LM curve shift to the left. The final result depends on the relative magnitudes of these shifts: if the former prevails, a point such as *C''*, corresponding to an increase in income, will be reached, while, if the latter is stronger, *C'* will be obtained.

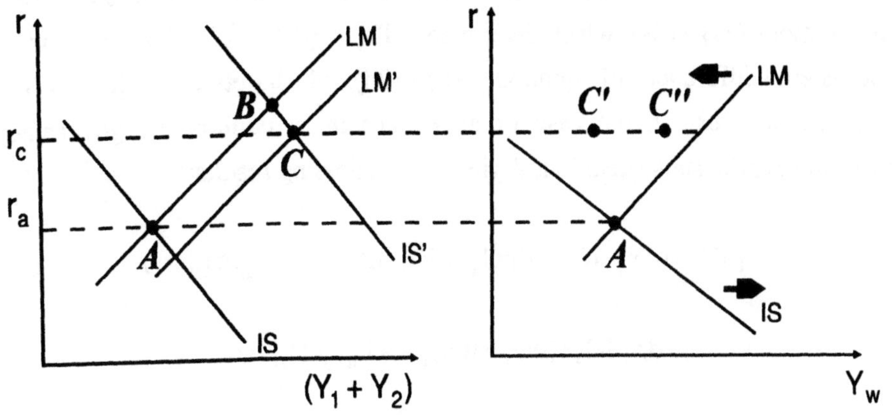

Fig. 12: The efficacy of fiscal policy under fixed exchange rates.

The results for the union are the same as in the "small" union fixed exchange rate case, while they differ from those found for the "small" union with flexible exchange rates towards the rest of the world, where the policy operation was expansionary for the country undertaking it and contractionary for the other union member, because of the prevailing contractionary effect of the exchange rate appreciation. The ambiguity of the result for the rest of the world resembles that of the two-country model with fixed exchange rates, which is, as already mentioned, a result of the symmetry assumption for the union member-countries, which behave as a single economic unit facing the rest of the world.

The multipliers of a rest of the world fiscal operation are:

$$(dY_1+dY_2)/dG_w = [2T_{uYw}(2L_{ur}+EL_{wr})-2C_{wr}L_{wYw}]/|D_1| \gtrless 0$$

$$dY_w/dG_w = [(1-C_{uYu}-T_{uYu})(2L_{ur}+EL_{wr})+C_{ur}L_{uYu}]/|D_1| > 0$$

$$dr/dG_w = - [2T_{uYw}L_{uYu+}(1\text{-}C_{uYu}\text{-}T_{uYu})EL_{wYw}]/|D_1| > 0.$$

II) Symmetry between the union member-countries and between the union as a whole and the rest of the world

The model will be now decomposed, as in section 6, into the subsystem "sum" of equations (1s) - (2s), which determines $[dY_w + (dY_1 + dY_2)]$ and dr, and the subsystem "difference" of equations (1d) - (2d), which determines $[dY_w - (dY_1 + dY_2)]$ and dR. In the case of an expansion in country 1's government expenditure, the subsystem "sum" yields the following results:

$$[dY_w+(dY_1+dY_2)]/[dG_w+(dG_1+dG_2)] = 4L_{ur}/|D_2| > 0$$

$$dr/[dG_w+(dG_1+dG_2)] = - L_{uYu}/|D_2| > 0$$

where $|D_2|$ is the same as in section 6.

The subsystem difference yields:

$$[dY_w\text{-}(dY_1+dY_2)]/[dG_w\text{-}(dG_1+dG_2)] = 2/|D_3| > 0$$

$$dR/[dG_w\text{-}(dG_1+dG_2)] = - L_{uYu}/|D_3| < 0$$

where $|D_3|$ is as in section 6.

Therefore one obtains that:

$$dY_w/dG_1 =$$

$$\tfrac{1}{2}\{[dY_w+(dY_1+dY_2)]/[dG_w+(dG_1+dG_2)]+[dY_w\text{-}(dY_1+dY_2)]/[dG_w\text{-}(dG_1+dG_2)]$$

$$= \tfrac{1}{2}\,[(4C_{ur}/|D_2|) - (2/|D_3|)] \gtrless 0$$

$(dY_1+dY_2)/dG_1=$

$$\tfrac{1}{2}\{[dY_w+(dY_1+dY_2)]/[dG_w+(dG_1+dG_2)]-[dY_w-(dY_1+dY_2)]/[dG_w-(dG_1+dG_2)]$$

$$= \tfrac{1}{2}\,[(4C_{ur}/|D_2|) - (-2/|D_3|)] > 0.$$

The result that a fiscal expansion in one of the union member-countries has a positive effect on the union income level and an uncertain one on that of the rest of the world is confirmed, as well as the rise in the world interest rate. The effects on reserves is such that those of the union increase and those of the rest of the world decrease, as one would have expected.

In the long run, instead, a domestic fiscal expansion is contractionary abroad: the increase in P_u worsens the consumer price index in the rest of the world, therefore leading to a decrease in the supply of labour for a given nominal wage (i. e., the ratio between P_u and EP_w increases and Y_w^s decreases).

Conclusions

This section summarizes the main results of the chapter for the short-run horizon and draws some conclusions concerning the single currency area optimality criteria in the "big" union case.

1) Efficacy of monetary policy

Under a regime of internationally flexible exchange rates, an expansionary monetary policy undertaken by the union has a positive effect on its income level, the transmission mechanism being the influence on the trade balance of the depreciation of the exchange rate towards the rest of the world, as it was in the "small" union case analysed in chapter II. The effect on the rest of the world income is, conversely, contractionary, while in the "small" union case this variable was exogenous to the model and therefore unaffected by the union policy operation. The world interest rate, which was also considered exogenous in chapter II, decreases as a result of the monetary expansion and the decrease in Y_w.

In the case of fixed exchange rates between the union and the rest of the world, the increase in the money supply of the union is redistributed between this and the rest of the world according to the tastes of the private asset holders and the changes in reserves necessary to keep the exchange rate at the fixed parity: both Y_u and Y_w, therefore, rise. In the "small" union case, instead, the change in M_u is not perceptible at the world money supply level and the union monetary policy is ineffective.

The change from a system of internationally fixed to one of internationally flexible exchange rates makes monetary policy a "beggar-thy-neighbour" instrument.

2) Efficacy of fiscal policy

A fiscal expansion in one of the two union member-countries has an expansionary effect on income in the country undertaking it and an uncertain effect in the other one. Such a result contrasts with the one obtained for the "small" union under a regime of flexible exchange rates: in that case, a fiscal expansion in one member country has a contractionary effect on the other one, as shown in chapter II. The difference between the two results is due to the endogeneity of the world variables in the "big" union case: the fiscal expansion causes an increase in the rest of the world income (through the improvement of the trade balance due to the appreciation of E) and in the world interest rate, which makes an increase of the level of income in the other union member-country compatible with equilibrium in the money market.

While under a flexible exchange rate regime an increase in government expenditure in the union is expansionary also in the rest of the world, it has an uncertain effect on Y_w under fixed exchange rates. This is due to the copresence of the expansionary trade linkage effect (the increse in Y_u induces an increase in the rest of the world exports) and the contractionary effect due to the loss of reserves necessary to counteract the downward pressure on E deriving from the fiscal expansion.

3) The "big" union and the optimality criteria

It has already been pointed out that the unification process brings about changes in the structural parameters of the economic system of the countries considered, so that the application of the optimality criteria should not refer to the pre-union situation. In particular, the variability of income, element influencing the mobility of the factors of production, as well as the production patterns of the countries, may change as a result of the unification process. Moreover, the role plyed by the non-member countries brings about elements which must be taken into account when trying to answer the question of the convenience for a country to join a monetary union.

The conclusions reached in chapter II are in some way strengthened in the case of a "big" union. This is true in particular for the income variability issue in the presence of real and monetary shocks hitting the union member-countries asymmetrically. As far as a shock to the real sector is concerned, the results on fiscal policy show that the loss of the flexibility of the exchange rate has in this case smaller negative consequences, and this for two main reasons: a) a shock hitting the real sector of a union member-country might be positively transmitted to the other even in the short run: this means that an element of divergence vanishes; b) the positive transmission to the rest of the world lowers the intensity of the need for an appreciation of the exchange rate and could even lead to a depreciation: this makes the long-run change in income smaller, even smaller than in the short run in the case of a depreciation, thus easing the task of a stabilizing policy response.

In the case of a shock hitting the monetary sector, the same considerations apply to the union member-countries as for the "small" union case, i. e. the intra-union fixed exchange rate system redistributes the effects of the disturbance between the two countries in the short run and in the medium run and neutralizes them in the long run.

Bibliography

Alogoskoufis, G.; Portes, R. (1991): "The International Costs and Benefits of EMU", *NBER Working Paper* Nr. 3384, June.

Aoki, M. (1981): *Dynamic Analysis of Open Economies*, New York, London, Toronto.

Canzoneri, M.; Henderson, D. (1991): *Monetary Policy in Interdependent Economies: A Game Theoretical Approach*, Cambridge (Mass.).

Feuerstein, S.; Siebke, J. (1990): "Wechselkursunion und Stabilitätspolitik", in: *Zeitschrift für Wirtschafts- und Sozialwissenschaften* 110, p. 359-370.

Goodhart, C. (1992): "The external Dimension of EMU", *LSE Financial Markets Group Special Paper* Nr. 42.

Gries, T. (1989): "Zum Problem internationalen Interdependenzen von Finanz- und Gütermärkten", Frankfurt a. M.

Herberg, H. (1991): "Terms of Trade and Welfare Effects of Quantitative Import Restrictions in a Three-Country World", *Diskussionbeiträge aus dem Institut für Theoretische Volkswirtschaftslehre*, Nr. 85, Universität Kiel.

Jarchow, H.-J. (1992): "Fiskalpolitik in einer Währungsunion", *Diskussionsbeiträge aus dem Volkswirtschaftlichen Seminar der Universität Göttingen*, Beitrag Nr. 58.

Levin, J. H. (1983): "A Model of Stabilization Policy in a Jointly Floating Currency Area", in: Bhandari, J. S.; Putnam, B. H. (eds), *Economic Interdependence and Flexible Exchange Rates*, Cambridge (Mass.), London, p. 329-349.

McKibbin, W. J.; Sachs, J. D. (1991): *Global Linkages: Macroeconomic Interdependence and Cooperation in the World Economy*, Washington, The Brookings Institution.

Salvatore, D. (1992): *European Integration and the Future of the International Monetary System*, Fordham University, mimeo.

Thomsen, U. (1992): "Stabilitätspolitik in einer kleinen Wechselkursunion bei festem externen Wechselkurs", in: *Diskussionbeiträge aus dem Institut für theoretische Volkswirtschaftslehre der Universität Kiel*, Nr. 90.

Wohltmann, H.-W. (1993): "Transmission nationaler Wirtschaftspolitiken in einer Wechselkursunion", *Jahrbücher für Nationalökonomie und Statistik* 211, p. 73-89.

Wohltmann, H.-W. (1994): "Die intertempolaren Auswirkungen antizipierter stabilisierungspolitischer Maßnahmen - Ein dynamischer Zwei-Länder-Ansatz", in: *Jahrbuch für Sozialwissenschaften*, Heft 1.

CHAPTER V
MONETARY AND FISCAL POLICY IN A "BIG" EXCHANGE RATE UNION
A STRATEGIC ANALYSIS

Introduction

In this chapter the strategic interactions between two countries forming an exchange rate union and the rest of the world are analysed. Each country pursues its targets using policy instruments, the change of which also affects the other countries' targets. The system of interdependence is derived from the model studied in chapter IV, the introductory section of which is to be referred to for references to the literature on the policy coordination debate. The medium-run results of the model will be used, as the most idenous for the purpose of analysing policy interactions.

The first three sections of this chapter analyse monetary policy. Section 1 illustrates the system of interdependence and the authority utility functions both in the case of flexible and fixed exchange rates. In section 2 the non-cooperative, cooperative and leadership solutions are derived. The results are commented in section 3. The last three sections concern fiscal policy. The system is presented in section 4 and solved in section 5 for the Nash, Pareto and Stackelberg outcomes, while section 6 summarizes the main results of the analysis.

1. Monetary policy: the system of interdependence and the authorities' utility functions

In this section a model describing the strategic interactions between two countries belonging to an exchange rate union and a third country, or rest of the world, is developed. Each country tries to minimize changes in the output and price levels using monetary policy. When a country changes its instrument, it affects not only its own targets, but also those of the other two countries. This interdependence, added to the fact that the number of targets (two) is bigger than that of available instruments (one), introduces scope for policy games between the three countries, once they are hit by exogenous shocks. It is assumed that the model underlying the system of interdependence is that developed in chapter IV. As a result of the simplifying assumptions introduced there, the two member countries are considered to react symmetrically to changes in the instrument; the money supply, moreover, is unique for the union as whole. Two distinct cases will be considered: (a) a flexible exchange rate regime exists between the union and the rest of the world; (b) a fixed exchange rate regime exists between the union and the rest of the world.

(a) Flexible exchange rates

The reduced form equations derived from chapter IV's model are the following (notation as in chapter III, all parameters positive):

(1a) $$dy_1 = i_1\, dm_u - a_1\, dm_w + dx$$

(2a) $$dy_2 = i_2\, dm_u - a_2\, dm_w + c_1\, dx$$

(3a) $$dy_w = a_w\, dm_w - i_w\, dm_u + c_2\, dx$$

(4a) $$dq_1 = w_1\, dm_u - b_1\, dm_w + c_w\, dx$$

(5a) $$dq_2 = w_2\, dm_u - b_2\, dm_w + f_1\, dx$$

(6a) $$dq_w = b_w\, dm_w - w_w\, dm_u + f_2\, dx.$$

Equation (1a) says that a change in country 1's output level can be induced by a change in the union money stock, an increase (decrease) in the latter causing an increase (decrease) in the former, by a change in the rest of the world money supply, the transmission being negative in this case, and by a shock hitting the economy. The same applies to equation (2a) for country 2 and symmetrically, to equation (3a) for the rest of the world. Equation (4a) describes how a change in country 1's consumer price index can be induced by a change in the union money supply, the relationship between the changes being positive, by a change in the rest of the world money supply, according to a negative relationship, and by an exogenous shock. The same applies to equation (5a) for country 2 and symmetrically to equation (6a) for the rest of the world.

The authorities are assumed to dislike changes both in the output and in the consumer price index. As far as the monetary union is concerned, being the money supply unique, also the decision about varying it is assumed to be unique, i. e. to be assigned to a unique monetary authority which maximizes a unique union utility function. It is assumed that the latter is a weighted sum of the member-countries' utility functions, the weights adding up to unity and assumed to be equal to ½. The arguments of the utility functions need not have the same importance relative to each other: in the following examples this will be expressed by a weight being given to changes in the output level, ß, so that, for $ß < 1$, one assumes that the authorities dislike inflation (deflation) relative more than changes in the output level. The utility functions for the union, U_u, and for the rest of the world, U_w, will then be expressed by:

(7) $$U_u = - \tfrac{1}{2}\, [ß(dy_1)^2 + (dq_1)^2] - \tfrac{1}{2}\, [ß(dy_2)^2 + (dq_2)^2]$$

(8) $$U_w = - [ß(dy_w)^2 + (dq_w)^2].$$

(b) Fixed exchange rates

For the case of fixed exchange rates, the system of interdependence is different, since changes in the money supply of either the union or the rest of the world are positively related with changes in the income and price levels. One therefore has:

(1b) $dy_1 = i_1\, dm_u + a_1\, dm_w + c_1\, dx$

(2b) $dy_2 = i_2\, dm_u + a_2\, dm_w + c_2\, dx$

(3b) $dy_w = a_w\, dm_w + i_w\, dm_u + c_w\, dx$

(4b) $dq_1 = w_1\, dm_u + b_1\, dm_w + f_1\, dx$

(5b) $dq_2 = w_2\, dm_u + b_2\, dm_w + f_2\, dx$

(6b) $dq_w = b_w\, dm_w + w_w\, dm_u + f_w\, dx.$

Given the symmetry assumption intoduced in chapter IV for the two union member-countries, the system of interdependence can be simplified as:

(1b') $(dy_1+dy_2) = i_u\, dm_u + a_u\, dm_w + c_u\, dx$

(2b') $dy_w = a_w\, dm_w + i_w\, dm_u + c_w\, dx$

(3b') $(dq_1+dq_2) = w_u\, dm_u + b_u\, dm_w + f_u\, dx$

(6b) $dq_w = b_w\, dm_w + w_w\, dm_u + f_w\, dx.$

Given the fixity of the exchange rate and the full mobility of capital, it is impossible to distinguish between the effects of dm_u and dm_w, since there exist a unique instrument the world money supply, i.e.:

$$i_u = a_u;$$
$$i_w = a_w;$$
$$w_u = b_u;$$
$$w_w = b_w.$$

In order to perform a strategic analysis, one must assume that the two money supplies are not perfect substitutes, i. e. because of some form of capital control still existing between the union and the rest of the world.

2. Monetary policy: the Nash, cooperative and Stackelberg solutions

(a) Flexible exchange rates

In order to solve the system one must first substitute for dy_1 and dy_2 from equations (1a) and (2a) and for dq_1 and dq_2 from equations (4a) and (5a) into equation (7), thus obtaining:

(9) $$U_u = -\tfrac{1}{2}[\beta(i_1 dm_u - a_1 dm_w + c_1 dx)^2 + (w_1 dm_u - b_1 dm_w + c_2 dx)^2] - \tfrac{1}{2}[\beta(i_2 dm_u - a_2 dm_w + f_1 dx)^2 + (w_2 dm_u - b_2 dm_w + f_2 dx)^2].$$

Making use of the symmetry assumption between the union member-countries, i. e. of the result that:

$$i_1 = i_2 = i_u;$$
$$a_1 = a_2 = i_u;$$
$$w_1 = w_2 = i_u;$$
$$b_1 = b_2 = i_u;$$
$$c_1 = c_2 = c_u;$$
$$f_1 = f_2 = f_u;$$

one gets:

$$(10) \qquad U_u = -[\beta(i_u dm_u - a_u dm_w + c_u dx)^2 + (w_u dm_u - b_u dm_w + f_u dx)^2].$$

Equation (10) is the formula for the union authorities' indifference curves, corresponding to an ellipses. The formula for the rest of the world indifference curves is obtained by substituting for dy_w from equation (3a) and for dp_w from equation (6a) into equation (8), thus obtaining:

$$(11) \qquad U_w = -[\beta(a_w dm_w - i_w dm_u + c_w dx)^2 + (b_w dm_w - w_w dm_u + f_w dx)^2].$$

Maximizing equation (10) with respect to dm_u and equation (11) with respect to dm_w, the reaction functions for the union, R_u, and for the rest of the world, R_w, are obtained. They indicate the optimal choice of the own instrument given the other country's choice:

$$(12) \quad R_u: \qquad dm_u = (l/a)\, dm_w - (c/a)\, dx$$

$$(13) \quad R_w: \qquad dm_w = (g/f)\, dm_u - (h/f)\, dx$$

where:

$$a = (\beta i_u^{\,2} + w_u^{\,2});$$
$$l = (\beta i_u a_u + w_u b_u);$$
$$c = (\beta i_u c_u + w_u f_u);$$
$$f = (\beta a_w^{\,2} + b_w^{\,2});$$
$$g = (\beta a_w i_w + b_w w_w);$$
$$h = (\beta a_w c_w + b_w f_w).$$

Assuming dx equal to zero, each country can set its instrument equal to zero and obtain its goals, as it can be seen from equations (10) and (11). In the presence of a shock, however, this is no longer true. If the shock affects the income and price levels negatively, i. e. $dx < 0$, and the indifference curves and reaction functions are drawn in the (dm_u, dm_w) space, the interception point of R_u with the dm_u axis has coordinates [0, (c/l)dx], that with the dm_w axis [-(c/a) dx, 0]; the corresponding interception points of R_w are [0, -(h/e)dx] and [(h/g)dx, 0]. The interception point between the two reaction functions, *N*, has coordinates dm_u = -[(lh+cf)/(af-gl)]dx and dm_w = -[(gc+ah)/(af-gl)]dx, which are positive if a > l, i. e. if $i_u > a_u$ and $w_u > b_u$, and if f > g, i. e. if $a_w > i_w$ and $b_w > w_w$, which is equivalent to the condition that the effect of a change in the domestic instrument is greater than that of a change in the foreign one. In this case *N* lies in the first quadrant.

The coordinates of the bliss point for the union, B_u, are found by setting $dy_1=dy_2=dq_1=dq_2=0$ in equations (1a), (2a), (4a), (5a), making use of the symmetry assumption and solving for dm_u and dm_w the system of equations (14) - (15):

$$i_u\, dm_u - a_u\, dm_w + c_u\, dx = 0 \tag{14}$$

$$w_u\, dm_u - b_u\, dm_w + f_u\, dx = 0 \tag{15}$$

which yields:

$$dm_u = [(a_u f_u - b_u c_u)/(b_u i_u - w_u a_u)]\, dx \gtrless 0$$

$$dm_w = [(i_u f_u - w_u c_u)/(w_u a_u - i_u b_u)]\, dx \gtrless 0$$

and symmetrically for B_w. The positions of the bliss points are undetermined, unless numerical values are given to the relevant parameters. As illustrated in chapter III, in the extreme case of the shock and the other country's instrument only affecting one target, B_u will be at the intersection point of R_u with the dm_w axis and B_w at the intersection point of the R_w with the dm_u axis. Since this case does not fit the model, it will be assumed that the bliss points lie to the left of *N*.

The picture corresponding to the above analysis is illustrated in Fig. 1. Point *N*, i. e. the intersection point between the two reaction functions, is the Nash equilibrium solution. It is Pareto dominated by the points contained in the shaded area, which can be reached only if the union and the rest of the world agree to cooperate, taking into account the negative spillover effects that their policy operations impose on each other. As previously mentioned in chapter III, this is possible only if an agreement on the distribution of the benefits is reached. Moreover, the cooperative solution, e. g. *C*, selected through this bargaining process being at least off the reaction function of one country, there will always be an incentive for at least one country not to stick to the agreement.

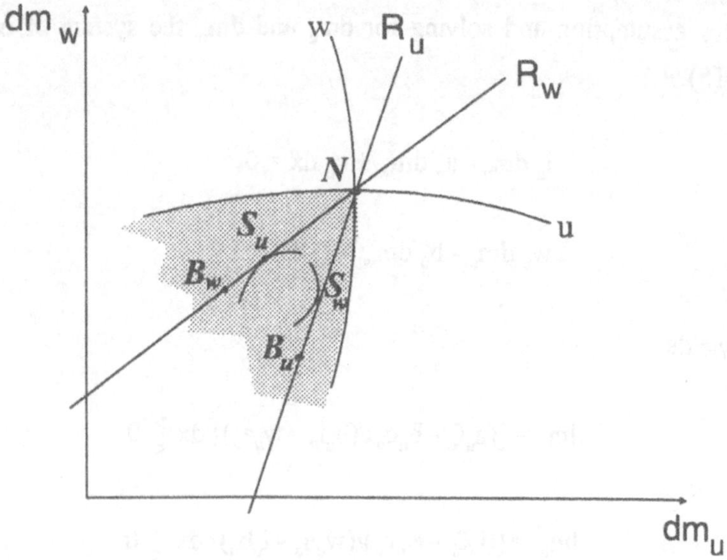

Fig. 1: The Nash, Pareto and Stackelberg solutions in the monetary policy game.

The cooperative solution corresponds to a smaller reaction of the countries to the shock affecting them: with both dm_u and dm_w varying less, income and the price level will also vary less, thus allowing the countries to reach a higher utility level.

It can also be noted that the model does not offer any incentive for a country to become a leader. This is the case when one country, knowing that the other one always follows its decision choosing a point on its reaction function, selects the value of its instrument corresponding to the point of tangency between one of its own indifference curves and the other country's reaction function. This equilibrium, called Stackelberg solution, always implies an incentive for the leader to move away, since it does not lie on its reaction function. In the case examined here, moreover, a country is better off as a follower than as a leader, as it can be seen by comparing point S_u, corresponding to the union acting as a leader, and point S_w, corresponding to the rest of the world being a leader.

The last question to be addressed is how the solution would differ if country 1 and country 2 did not cooperate with each other, as assumed up to this point. This would mean that each country maximizes its own utility function over its own instrument, i. e. that country 1 maximizes equation 5.16:

(16) $$U_1 = -[ß(dy_1)^2 + (dq_1)^2,$$

subject to the following constraints:

(17) $$dy_1 = i_1\, dm_1 + j_1\, dm_2 - a_1\, dm_w + c_1\, dx$$

(18) $$dp_1 = w_1\, dm_1 + v_1\, dm_2 - b_1\, dm_w + c_2\, dx$$

which yields the reaction function for country 1, R_1:

(19) R_1: $$dm_1 = -(q/a)dm_2 + (b/a)dm_w - (c/a)dx$$

where:

$$q = (ßi_1j_1 + w_1v_1).$$

In the same way one obtains the reaction function for country 2, R_2:

(20) R_2: $$dm_2 = -(q/a)dm_1 + (b/a)dm_w - (c/a)dx.$$

Assuming then that the two union member countries are completely symmetrical and that $dm_1 = dm_2 = dm$, adding R_1 and R_2 and dividing by 2, one obtains the aggregate reaction function for the two countries when they are not cooperating, R_n (see Canzoneri/Henderson (1991)):

(21) R_n: $dm = (b/a+q)dm_w - (c/a+1)dx.$

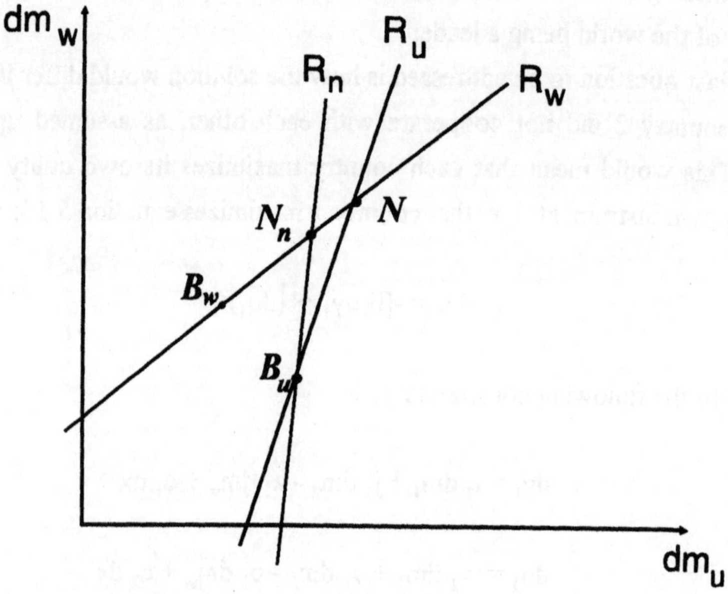

Fig. 2: The higher utility of the Nash equilibrium for the non-cooperative union (solution N_n), compared with the cooperative union (solution N).

In fig. 2 the equilibrium corresponding to country 1 and country 2 playing Nash with each other and then together with the rest of the world is shown by point N_n. It corresponds to a higher utility level for the aggregation of country 1 and country 2 than point N, i. e. the equilibrium point in the case of the two union member-countries cooperating with each other and playing Nash with the rest of the world.

This means that, if the union does not cooperate with the rest of the world, country 1 and country 2 are better off when they do not cooperate with each other than when they do. This is because the spillover effect between the two union member-countries and that between the union and the rest of the world have opposite signs and therefore tend to cancel each other when they are not taken into account by the countries when selecting the optimal values of their instruments.

(b) Fixed exchange rates

How is the analysis modified in the case of a fixed exchange rate between the union and the rest of the world? The system of interdependence consists now of equations (1b) - (6b). The union maximizes (7) over dm_u subject to equations (1b), (2b), (4b) and (5b), which yields the following reaction function, R_u':

(22) R_u': $$dm_u = -(b/a)dm_w - (c/a)dx$$

where the parameters are the same as above. The intersection point of the R_u' with the dm_u axis has coordinates [0, -(c/b)dx], that with the dm_w axis [-(c/a) dx, 0]. The bliss point for the union, B_u, is found by setting $dy_1 = dy_2 = 0$ in equation (1b)' and $dq_1 = dq_2 = 0$ in equation (3b)' and solving this two-equation system for dm_u and dm_w, which yields:

$$dm_u = -[(a_u f_u - i_u c_u)/(w_u a_u - i_u b_u)]\, dx$$

$$dm_w = -[(i_u f_u - w_u c_u)/(w_u a_u - i_u b_u)]\, dx.$$

The position of B_u depends on the values assumed by the parameters appearing in its coordinates. One can consider the case of one target being affected only by the domestic instrument as a reference point. Then, B_u will lie at the intersection point of R_u' with the dm_w axis.

The rest of the world maximizes equation (8) over dm_w subject to equations (2b)' and (4b)', which yields the following reaction function, R_w':

(23) R_w': $$dm_w = -(g/f)dm_u - (h/f)dx$$

where the parameters are the same as above.

The intersection point between R_w' and the dm_u axis has coordinates [0, -(h/f) dx], that with the dm_w axis [-(h/g)dx, 0]. The bliss point of the rest of the world, B_w, is found by setting $dy_w = dq_w = 0$ in equations (2b)' and (4b)' and solving this two-equation system for dm_u and dm_w, which yields:

$$dm_u = (a_w f_w - b_w c_w)/(b_w i_w - a_w w_w)$$

$$dm_w = -(i_w f_w - w_w c_w)/(b_w i_w - a_w w_w).$$

The exact position of B_w depends on the values taken by the parameters appearing in its coordinates: for instance, if one target is affected by the rest of the world instrument only, B_w will lie at the intersection point of R_w' and the dm_u axis. The intersection point between the two reaction functions, N, has coordinates {[(lh-cf)/(fa-gl)]dx, [(gc-ah)/(fa-gl)]dx}, found by solving the system formed by the equations of the two reaction functions for dm_u and dm_w. Point N lies in the first quadrant if the own policy effects are stronger than the foreign ones.

This analysis can be translated into the (dm_u, dm_w) space representation of Fig. 3. Point N is the Nash equilibrium solution, which is Pareto dominated since at least one country could be better off moving to a point in the shaded area. The non-cooperative solution, in fact, corresponds to a monetary response which is not enough expansionary, since the countries do not internalize the effect deriving from the foreign policy operation. Note that this result is obtained only if the Nash equilibrium point lies to the left of the bliss points. The usual considerations apply to the cooperative solution: a Pareto efficient outcome can be reached only if the countries agree to cooperate, which implies that they also agree on how the benefits deriving from cooperation should be distributed between them. The model does not offer incentives to stick to the agreed upon solution, on the contrary, being this, e. g. point C, off the reaction functions, each country has an incentive to move away from it.

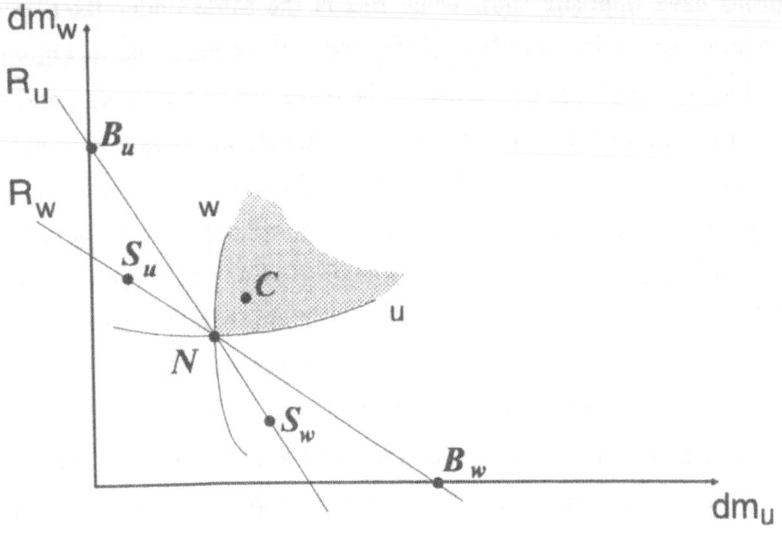

Fig. 3: The monetary policy coordination game under fixed exchange rates.

Another kind of equilibrium is the Stackelberg solution. If the union (rest of the world) acts as a leader, this is shown by point S_u (S_W) in Fig. 3. The leader is better off than in *N*, but has an incentive to move away because it is not on its reaction function. Moreover, there are no incentives to act as a follower either, since the utility would be lower than in the Nash equilibrium position.

3. Conclusions on monetary policy

The analysis developed in the preceding sections can be useful in studying the effects of the change from a fixed to a flexible exchange rate regime on international monetary policy coordination. In particular, as for the Nash equilibrium, it was shown that the policy response to an exogenous shock is too strong in the first case and too weak in the second one, the reason being that under flexible exchange rates the spillover effects on each union member-country deriving from the other member and the rest of the world policy operations have opposite sign, while this is the same under fixed exchange rates. Moreover, under flexible exchange rates there exists no incentive to act as a leader, since a player would always be better off as a follower, and there is also no incentive for the union member-countries to cooperate with each other if they are not cooperating with the rest of the world either. The flexible exchange rate regime, therefore, calls for less coordination by its very nature.

The result that the intra-union coordination of monetary policies might be "bad" does not apply to the case of a small union, with the rest of the world being unaffected by changes in the union money supply and therefore not reacting to them (which also has the consequence that the reaction to an exogenous shock is smaller than optimal and not too large as in the big union case, where the union also reacts to the negative spillover effects from the rest of the world). This qualifies the argument that a monetary union would be the more viable, the larger its influence on the rest of the world economic variables: in the case of flexible exchange rates, the lack of coordination with the rest of the world introduces a disruptive force into the union, since the members would be better off not coordinating their monetary policies and letting the intra-union positive spillover effects cancel the negative ones coming from the rest of the world.

4. Fiscal policy: the system of interdependence and the authorities' utility functions

In this section the strategic interactions between two countries forming an exchange rate union and another country which represents the rest of the world will be developed on the basis of chapter IV's model. Both the case of a flexible and that of a fixed exchange rate regime between the union and the rest of the world will be analysed.

It is assumed that each country targets income and the trade balance under flexible exchange rates and income and reserves under fixed exchange rates, using one policy instrument, the change in the level of government expenditure. The change of the instrument affects not only the own targets, but also those of the other countries. The copresence of these two conditions, i. e.

a higher number of targets than of available instruments and the interdependence between the countries makes scope for policy games.

(a) Flexible exchange rates

The system of interdependence for the flexible exchange rate case can be represented by the following reduced form equations:

(24a) $$dy_1 = a_1\, dg_1 \pm b_1\, dg_2 + c_1\, dg_w + dx$$

(25a) $$dy_2 = a_2\, dg_2 \pm b_2\, dg_1 + c_2\, dg_w + dx$$

(26a) $$dy_w = a_w\, dg_1 + b_w\, dg_2 + c_w\, dg_w + dx$$

(27a) $$dB_1 = -\, h_1\, dg_1 + k_2\, dg_2 + j_1\, dg_w + dx$$

(28a) $$dB_2 = -\, h_2\, dg_2 + k_1\, dg_1 + j_2\, dg_W + dx$$

(29a) $$dB_W = f_1\, dg_1 + f_2\, dg_2 - h_w\, dg_w + dx$$

where notation is as usual and all parameters are positive. Equations (24a) - (26a) say that a change in each country income level can be induced by a change in the level of government expenditure in any country and by a shock. Equations (27a) - (29a) are derived as follows: B_1 can be decomposed into its two components, B_{12}, the trade balance with country 2, and B_{1w}, the trade balance with the rest of the world. In the same way B_2 can be decomposed into B_{21} and B_{2w}, with $B_{21} = -B_{12}$, and B_w into B_{w1}, which is equal to $-B_{1w}$, and B_{w2}, which is equal to $-B_{2w}$. Changes in the trade balance between two countries are induced by changes in the level of government expenditure in either country:

(30) $$dB_{12} = -dB_{21} = -k_1 dg_1 + k_2 dg_2$$

(31) $$dB_{1w} = -dB_{w1} = -f_1 dg_1 + j_1 dg_w$$

(32) $$dB_{2w} = -dB_{w2} = -f_2 dg_2 + j_2 dg_w.$$

Setting then $(k_i + f_i) = h_i$ and substituting, one obtains equations (27a) - (29a).

The next step is to introduce the authorities' utility functions. It is assumed that countries dislike changes in the income level and in the trade balance, so that the utility functions of country 1, U_1, country 2, U_2 and the rest of the world, U_w, are:

(33) $$U_1 = -(dy_1)^2 - \beta_1(dB_1)^2$$

which must be maximized over dg_1, given dg_2 and dg_w, subject to (24a) and (27a);

(34) $$U_2 = -(dy_2)^2 - \beta_2(dB_2)^2$$

which must be maximized over dg_2, given dg_1 and dg_w, subject to equations (25a) and (28a);

(35) $$U_w = -(dy_w)^2 - \beta_w(dB_w)^2$$

which must be maximized over dg_w, given dg_1 and dg_2 and subject to equations (26a) and (29a).

In order to allow a bidimensional representation of the system, the equations referring to the union member-countries will be grouped together. This can be done in two ways:

1) The two countries are assumed to target $(dy_1+dy_2) = dy_u$ and $(dB_1+dB_2) = dB_u$ by means of the instrument $(dg_1+dg_2) = dg_u$. The interdependence system then becomes:

(36a) $$dy_u = a_u dg_u + b_u dg_w + dx$$

(37a) $$dy_w = a_w dg_w + b_w dg_u + dx$$

(38a) $$dB_u = -dB_w = -c_u dg_u + l_u dg_w + dx$$

while the authorities' utility functions become:

(39a) $$U_u = -(dy_u)^2 - ß_u(dB_u)^2$$

(40a) $$U_w = -(dy_w)^2 - ß_w(-dB_u)^2.$$

2) If the two union member-countries are not assumed to cooperate, one can still derive an aggregate reaction function for the union by assuming that the two members have symmetric reactions to changes in the instruments and to shocks, adding the two reaction functions obtained for country 1 and country 2 and setting $dg_1 = dg_2$.

(b) Fixed exchange rates

In the case of fixed exchange rates between the union and the rest of the world, the system of interdependence becomes:

(24b) $$dy_1 = a_1 dg_1 + b_1 dg_2 \pm c_1 dg_w + dx$$

(25b) $$dy_2 = a_2 dg_2 + b_2 dg \pm c_2 dg_w + dx$$

(26b) $$dy_w = \pm a_w dg_1 \pm b_w dg_2 + c_w dg_w + dx$$

(27b) $$dR_1 = h_1 dg_1 - k_2 dg_2 - j_1 dg_w$$

(28b) $$dR_2 = h_2 dg_2 - k_1 dg_1 - j_2 dg_w$$

(29b) $$dR_w = -f_1 dg_1 - f_2 dg_2 + h_w dg_w.$$

The sign of the transmission of a fiscal policy operation between either union member-country and the rest of the world could be positive or negative, as shown in chapter IV, which is to be referred to also for the sign of the effect on reserves of a rise in government expenditure (equations (27b) - (29b) are derived in the same way as equations (27a) - (29a)).

The authorities' utility functions become:

(33b) $$U_1 = -(dy_1)^2 - ß_1(dR_1)^2$$

(34b) $$U_2 = -(dy_2)^2 - ß_2(dR_2)^2$$

(35b) $$U_w = -(dy_w)^2 - ß_w(dR_w)^2.$$

A two dimension graphical representation of the model can be done only considering the union as a unique entity, which can be done in two ways:

1) If one assumes that the two union member-countries cooperate with each other, then the interdependence system and the authorities' utility functions become:

(36b) $$dy_u = a_u dg_u \pm b_u dg_w + dx$$

(37b) $$dy_w = a_w dg_w \pm b_w dg_u + dx$$

(38b) $$dR_u = -dR_w = c_u dg_u - l_u dg_w$$

(39b) $$U_u = -(dy_u)^2 - ß_u(dR_u)^2$$

(40b) $$U_w = -(dy_w)^2 - ß_w(-dR_u)^2.$$

2) If the two union member-countries do not cooperate, one can still construct an aggregate union reaction function by adding those of the two members, assuming that they have symmetric reactions to changes in the instruments and to the shock, as well as the same preferences.

5. Fiscal policy: the Nash, cooperative and Stackelberg solutions

(a) Flexible exchange rates

In order to solve the system presented in the previous section, the first step is finding the reaction functions for the union R_u, and for the rest of the world, R_w. R_u is obtained by substituting for dy_u and dB_u in equation (39a) from equations (36a) and (38a) respectively and maximizing over dg_u, given dg_w and dx:

(41) R_u: $$dg_u = - (n/m)\, dg_w - (a_u/m)\, dx$$

where:

$$m = (a_u^2 + \beta_u c_u^2);$$

$$n = (a_u b_u - \beta_u c_u l_u).$$

In the (dg_u, dg_w) space, the intercept of R_u with the dg_u axis has coordinates [(-a_u/m)dx, 0), that with the dg_w axis [0, (- a_u/n)dx]. The bliss point for the union, B_u, is found by putting $dy_u = dB_u = 0$ in equations (36a) and (38a) and solving this two-equation system for dg_u and dg_w, which yields coordinates {[-l_u/ ($l_u a_u + c_u b_u$)]dx, [-c_u/ ($l_u a_u + c_u b_u$)] dx}.

The reaction function for the rest of the world is found by substituting for dy_w and dB_u in equation 5.40(a) from equations (37a) and (38a), thus obtaining:

(42) R_w: $$dg_w = - (s/q)\, dg_u - (a_w/q)\, dx$$

where:

$$q = (a_w^2 + \beta_w l_u^2);$$

$$s = (a_w b_w - \beta_w l_u c_u).$$

The intercept of R_w with the dg_u axis has coordinates $\{[-a_w/(a_w b_w - ß_w l_u c_u)]dx, 0\}$, that with the dg_w axis $\{0, [-a_w/ (a_w^2 + +ß_w l_u^2)]dx\}$. The bliss point for the rest of the world, B_w, is found by putting $dy_w = - dB_u = 0$ in equations (36a) and (38a) and solving this two equation system for dg_u and dg_w, which yields coordinates equal to $\{[-l_u/(l_u a_w+c_u b_u)]dx, [-c_u/(l_u a_w+c_u b_u)]dx\}$.

The reaction functions are downward sloping if ß is small and the bliss points lie both on the same side of the 45° line (to the left of it for $c_u > l_u$ and viceversa), as a result of the fact that the trade balances of the countries are the opposite of each other. The interception point between R_u and R_w, *N*, which corresponds to the Nash solution, is found by solving the system formed by the two reaction functions for dg_u and dg_w, which yields:

$$dg_u = [(a_w n - a_u q)/(qm-sn)]dx$$

$$dg_w = [(a_u s - a_w m)/(qm-sn)]dx.$$

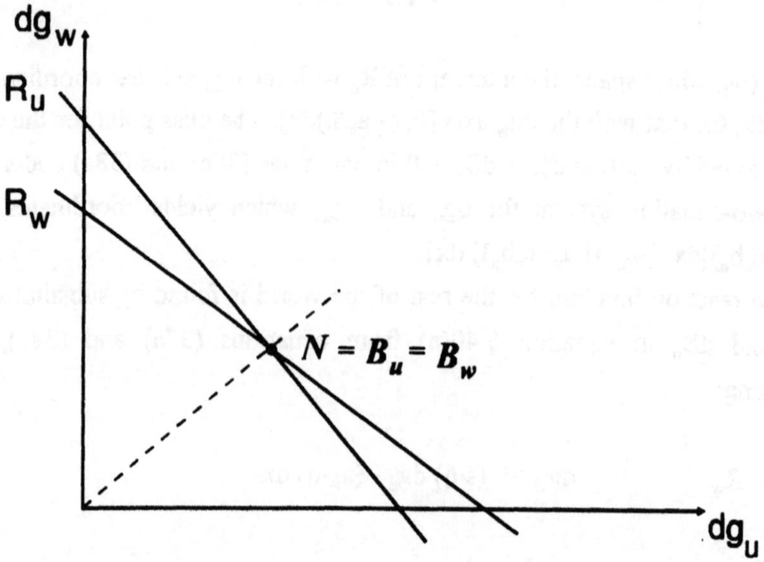

Fig. 4: The coincidence of the Nash equilibrium with the bliss points wehn the union and the rest of the world are mirror images.

As in the cases previously analysed, in the absence of a shock both the union and the rest of the world can reach their bliss points by setting the change in the level of government expenditure equal to zero. In this case, however, there is another situation in which each country can reach its bliss point even in the presence of a shock, i. e. when they are one the mirror image of the other. This is a consequence of the reduction of the number of targets at the aggregate level, the foreign one being unique since both the union and the rest of the world want $dB_u = 0$. Setting $a_u = a_w = b_u = b_w = a$ in R_u and R_w, one obtains that the reaction functions have reciprocal slopes and that $B_u = B_w = N$, the coordinates being [-1/2a)dx, (-1/2a)dx], which means that they lie on the 45° line (see Fig. 4).

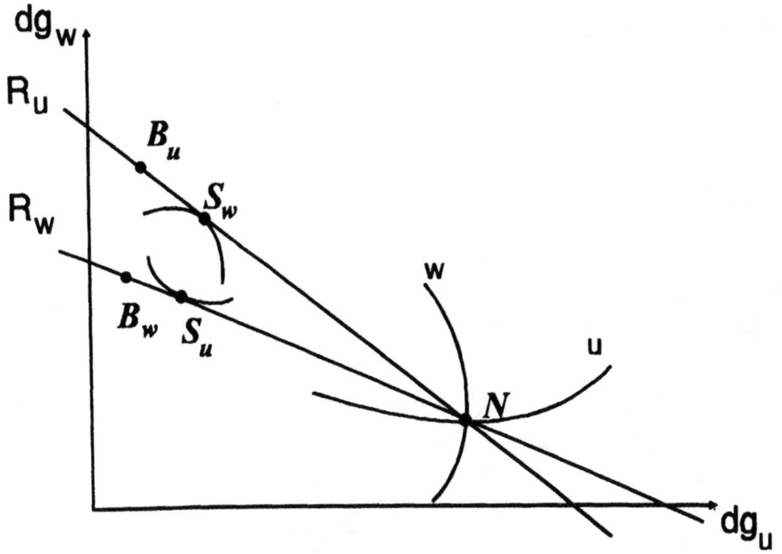

Fig. 5: The non-cooperative response to a negative shock of the country having the stronger (smaller) impact on the external target is too (not enough) expansionary.

If the union and the rest of the world are not assumed to react symmetrically, the bliss points do not coincide any more in the presence of a shock. Their position with respect to the Nash equilibrium point varies with the values of the parameters of the system and of the relative weights of the targets. Fig. 5, drawn, as usual, for a negative shock, shows the case of the bliss points being both above the 45° line and to the left of *N*: then, the non-cooperative solution corresponds to a too expansionary response of the country whose policy instrument has a stronger effect on the external target, the union in the example, and to a not enough expansionary one of the rest of the world. In this situation both countries would be better off in the Stackelberg equilibrium points (S_u if the union leads, S_w if the rest of the world does) than in *N*, but each country is better off as a follower than as a leader.

Fig. 6 shows a case in which the non-cooperative solution is too expansionary for both countries, which applies when the weights attached to the external targets are not very small. If the external target is set at a very low level, the bliss points might be in the opposite positions, with respect to *N*, of those shown in the figures, and then the non-cooperative solution would show a contractionary bias.

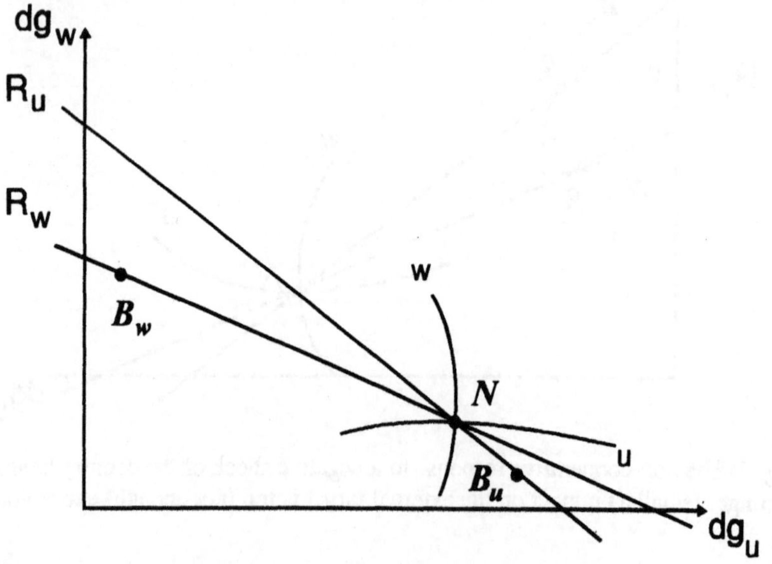

Fig. 6: In the case of a relatively large weight attached to the external target, the Nash equilibrium shows an expansionary bias.

What happens if the two union member-countries do not cooperate with each other? In this case country 1 maximizes (33) over dg_1 subject to (24a) and (26a), while country 2 maximizes (34) over dg_2 subject to (25a) and (27a) and therefore a distinction must be drawn between the case of a positive and that of a negative intra-union transmission.

In the case of a positive intra-union transmission, the reaction function for country 1, R_1, is the following:

(43) $$R_1{:}dg_1=-[(a_1b_1-\beta_1h_1k_2)/(a_1^2+\beta_1h_1^2)]dg_2-[(a_1c_1-\beta_1h_1j_1)/(a_1^2+\beta_1h_1^2)]dg_w-[(a_1+\beta h_1)/(a_1^2+\beta_1h_1^2)]dx$$

and similarly for R_2.

Assuming that the two countries are mirror images, denoting the parameters with the subscript "u", adding R_1 and R_2 and setting $dg_1 = dg_2 = dg_u$ yields the aggregate reaction function for the two countries, R_u^n:

(44) $$R_u^n{:}dg_u=-[(a_uc_u-\beta_uh_uj_u)/(a_u^2+\beta_uh_u^2+a_ub_u-\beta_uh_uk_u)dg_w-[(a_u-\beta h_u)/(a_u^2+\beta_uh_u^2+a_ub_u-\beta_uh_uk_u)]\ dx.$$

If the intra-union transmission is negative, R_1 becomes:

(43') $$R_1{:}dg_1 = [(a_1b_1+\beta_1h_1k_2)/(a_1^2+\beta_1h_1^2)]dg_2-[(a_1c_1-\beta_1h_1j_1)/(a_1^2+\beta_1h_1^2)]dg_w-[(a_1+\beta h_1)/(a_1^2+\beta_1h_1^2)]\ dx$$

and similarly for R_2.

Assuming that the two countries are mirror images, denoting the parameters with the subscript u, adding R_1 and R_2 and setting $dg_1 = dg_2 = dg_u$ yields the aggregate reaction function for the two countries, R_u^n:

(44') $$R_u^n{:}dg_u=-[(a_uc_u-\beta_uh_uj_u)/(a_u^2+\beta_uh_u^2+a_ub_u+\beta_uh_uk_u)dg_w-[(a_u-\beta h_u)/(a_u^2+\beta_uh_u^2+a_ub_u+\beta_uh_uk_u)]\ dx.$$

R_u^n is flatter than R_u with respect to the dg_u axis. Therefore, the new Nash equilibrium point, N^n, corresponds to a higher utility level than N, as shown in

Fig. 6 bis, which means that the member-countries are better off if they do not cooperate with each other, provided that no cooperation with the rest of the world takes place. This is a consequence of the fact that the intra-union negative spillover effects tend to offset the external positive ones.

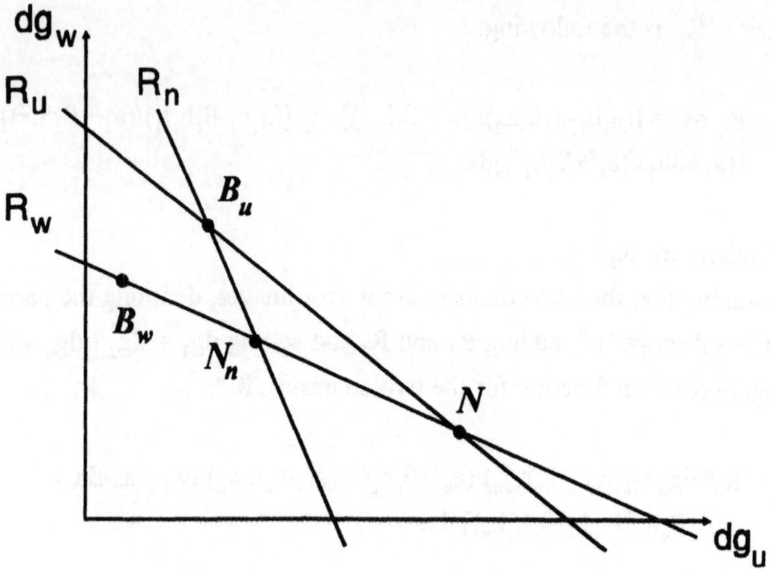

Fig. 6 bis: The higher utility of the Nash equilibrium for the non-cooperative union (Nn) with respect to the cooperative one (N).

(b) Fixed exchange rates.

In the case of fixed exchange rates between the union and the rest of the world, the system of interdependence could be either positive or negative, as far as income is concerned. In what follows the latter case will be considered, in order to differentiate the analysis from the flexible exchange rate one, thus obtaining positively sloped reaction functions.

In the case of the two union member-countries cooperating with each other, the union maximizes equation (39b) over dg_u subject to equations (36b) and (38b). Such an operation yields its reaction function, R_w:

(45) $$dg_u = (n/m)dg_w - (a/m_u)dx$$

where:

$$m = (a_u^2+\beta_u c_u^2);$$

$$n = (a_u b_u+\beta_u c_u l_u).$$

The interception points between R_u and the dg_u and dg_w axes have coordinates $[(-a_u/m)dx, 0]$ and $[0, (a_u/n)dx]$ respectively. The coordinates of the bliss point, B_u, are found by solving the system of equations (36b) and (38b) for dg_u and dg_w with $dy_u = dB_u = 0$, which yields:

$$dg_u = -[l_u/(l_u a_u - c_u b_u)]dx;$$

$$dg_w = -[c_u/(l_u a_u - c_u b_u)]dx.$$

The reaction function for the rest of the world, R_w, is found by maximizing equation (40b) over dg_w after substituting for dy_w from equation (37b) and for $-dR_u$ from equation (38b), thus obtaining:

(46) R_w: $$dg_w = (s/q)dg_u - (a_u/q)dx$$

where:

$$q = (a_w^2+\beta_w l_u^2);$$

$$s = (a_w b_w+\beta_w c_u l_u).$$

The interception points of R_w with the dg_u and dg_w axes have coordinates $[(a_w/s)dx, 0]$ and $[0, (-a_w/q)dx]$. The bliss point B_w is found by solving the system of equations (37b) and (38b) for dg_w and dg_u after setting $dy_w = dR_u = 0$, which yields:

$$dg_u = -[l_u/(l_u a_w - bwc_u)]dx;$$

$$dg_w = -[c_u/(l_u a_u - c_u b_w)]dx.$$

It can be seen that the reaction functions are upward sloping and that the bliss points lie on the same side with respect to the 45° line.

The intersection point between R_u and R_w, which corresponds to the Nash solution, is found by solving the system formed by the two reaction functions for dg_u and dg_w, thus obtaining:

$$dg_u = -[(a_u q + a_w n)/(qm - sn)]dx;$$

$$dg_w = -[(a_u s + a_w m)/(qm - sn)]dx;$$

which are positive if the domestic policy effect on income is stronger than the foreign one, in the case of a negative shock.

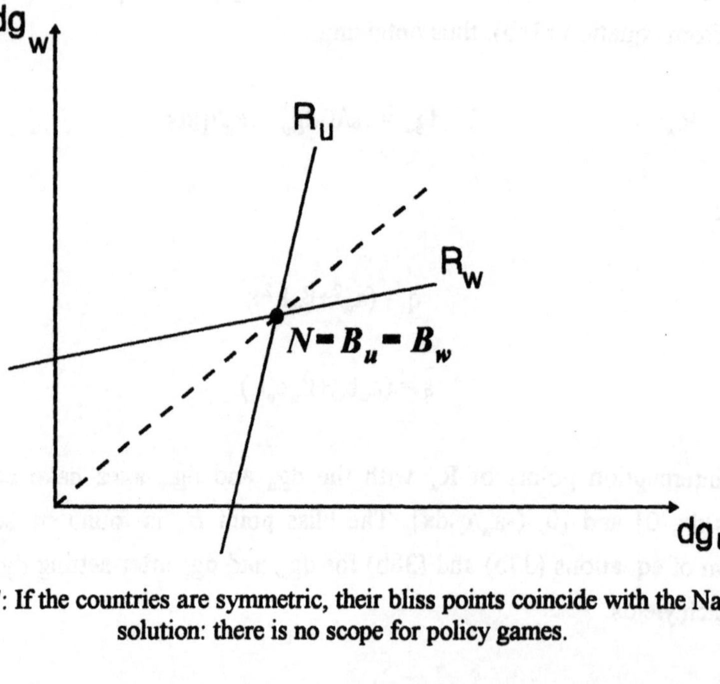

Fig. 7: If the countries are symmetric, their bliss points coincide with the Nash solution: there is no scope for policy games.

If no shock is hitting the two economies, each country can achieve its targets by setting the change in the level of government expenditure equal to zero. As in the flexible exchange rate case, if the countries are symmetric, the bliss points coincide and are also equal to the Nash solution of the system, the coordinates being both equal to -(1/2a)dx. In this case, represented in Fig. 7, there is no scope for policy games.

If the union and the rest of the world are not mirror images, the Nash solution will be Pareto dominated. Whether the Pareto improving points correspond to a too big or too little fiscal expansion depends on the position of the bliss points with respect to the Nash equilibrium. Fig. 8 shows the case of the non-cooperative solution having an expansionary bias: both countries could be better off by reducing their response to the contractionary shock. However, at least one country would have an incentive to move away from any agreed upon cooperative solution, being off its reaction function.

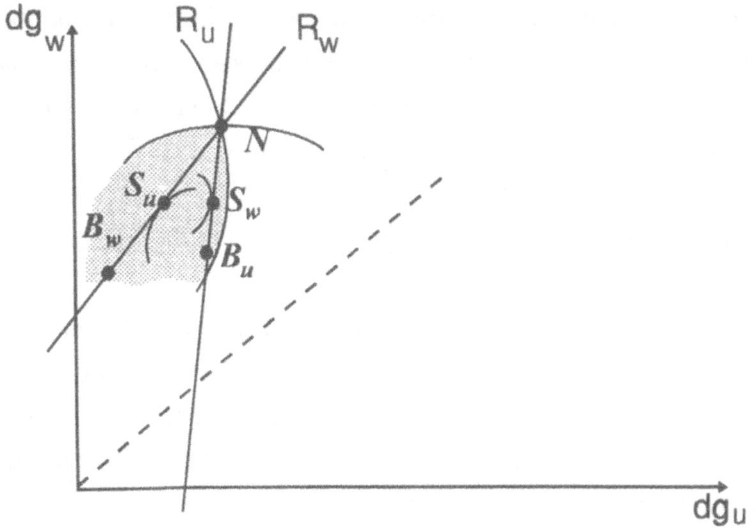

Fig. 8: The case of the non-cooperative solution showing an expansionary bias.

By the same token, even if the Stackelberg solution dominates the Nash equilibrium, there is no incentive for a country to be a leader, not only because it would then be off its reaction function, but also because it would be worse off than being a follower, as can be seen by comparing the utility of the union and of the rest of the world in point S_u, for the case of the union leading, and S_w for the rest of the world leading.

If the two union member-countries do not cooperate, one can still obtain an aggregate reaction function for the union as a whole by imposing the assumption that the members react symmetrically to changes in the instrument and to shocks, adding their two reaction functions and dividing by 2. The reaction function of country 1 is obtained by maximizing equation (33b) over dg_1 subject to equations (24b) and (27b):

(47) $R_1{:}dg_1 = -[(a_1b_1 - ß_1h_1k_2)/(a_1^2 + ß_1h_1^2)]dg_2 + [(a_1c_1 + ß_1h_1j_1)/(a_1^2 + ß_1h_1^2)]$ $dg_w - a_1dx.$

The reaction function of country 2 is obtained in a similar way and is the same as R_1 with subscripts 2 instead of 1. Assuming that the parameters describing the reaction to the domestic instrument, the foreign instrument and the shock, and the weights attached to the targets are the same for the two members, adding the two reaction functions and dividing by 2 one obtains the aggregate reaction function R_u^n:

(48) R_u^n: $dg_u = [(a_uc_u - ß_uh_uj_u)/(a_u^2 + ß_uh_u^2)]dg_w - [a_1/(a_u^2 + ß_uh_u^2)]dx$

which is flatter than the R_u with respect to the dg_u axis. Therefore the new Nash equilibrium point, N_n, corresponds to a higher aggregated utility level than N, as shown in Fig. 9, which means that the member-countries are better off if they do not cooperate, provided that no cooperation with the rest of the world takes place. This is a consequence of the fact that the intra-union positive spillover effects tend to offset the external negative ones.

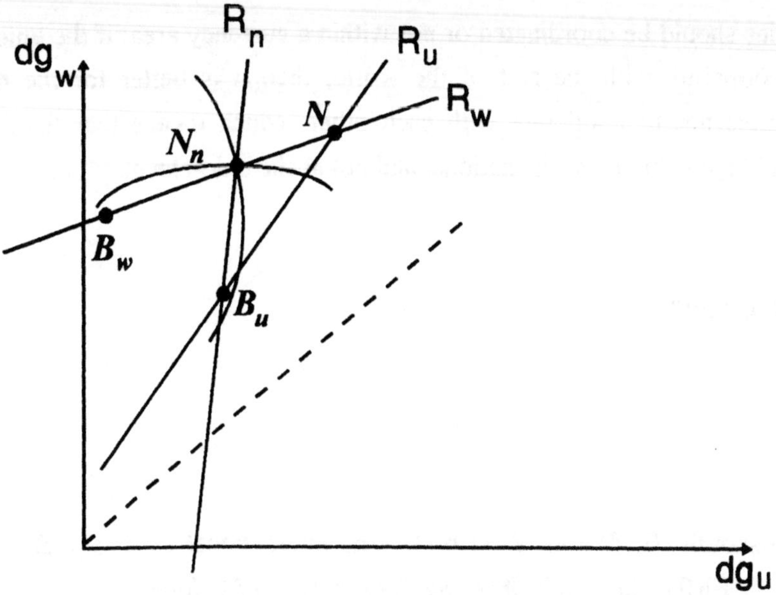

Fig. 9: The two union member-countries are better off not cooperating with each other, provided that no cooperation with the rest of the world takes place.

6. Conclusions on fiscal policy.

The reduction of the targets from four to three, due to the fact that the trade balance of the union and of the rest of the world are one the opposite of the other, makes it complicated to analyse the policy interactions between them, since either the bliss points are obtained, as in the symmetric case, or it is difficult to establish their exact position with respect to the Nash equilibrium point, so that one can determine whether the non-cooperative solution presents a contractionary or expansionary bias only introducing assumptions on the size of the parameters.

However, it has been shown that the non-cooperative solution is Pareto dominated both under flexible and under fixed exchange rates, but that the efficient solutions are such that the countries would be tempted to move away from them.

Finally, when the intra-union and external spillover effects have opposite sign, the model provides a definite answer to the question of whether fiscal policies should be coordinated or not within a currency area: if the union does not cooperate with the rest of the world, then it is better for the member countries not to cooperate with each other, which means that fiscal policy should be conducted at the national and not at the union level.

Bibliography

Alogoskoufis, G.; Portes, R. (1991): "The International Costs and Benefits of EMU", in: *NBER Working Papers*, Nr. 3884, June.

Canzoneri, M.; Henderson, D. (1991): *Monetary Policy in Interdependent Economies: A Game Theoretical Approach*, Cambridge (Mass.).

Goodhart, C. (1992): "The External Dimension of EMU", in : *LSE Financial Markets Group Special Papers*, Nr. 42.

CONCLUSIONS

The purpose of this work was to analyse the effects of monetary and fiscal policies undertaken by an exchange rate union member-country on its own macroeconomic performance, that of the rest of the union and of the countries not belonging to it; the possibility of improving this performance by policy coordination; and the influence that this exerts on the union cohesion.

These three aspects have been treated on the basis of a three-country IS-LM-AS model, from which the system of macroeconomic interdependence has been derived and then used for the analysis of policy coordination. The results have then been interpreted with particular reference to the question of the union cohesion.

It has been shown that **monetary policy** is positively transmitted within the union in the short run and in the medium run, while the usual policy inefficacy result applies for the long run. With flexible exchange rates between the union and the rest of the world, the transmission mechanism is the sensitivity of the trade balance to changes in the exchange rate; therefore, the country with a higher sensitivity, typically the relatively small country, experiences a greater change in the level of income. This qualifies the argument according to which it is the more convenient for a country to join an exchange rate union, the higher its degree of openness to foreign trade is: if the trade balance is very sensitive also to changes in the exchange rate towards the rest of the world, the blocking of parities with the other union members has only limited stabilization effects.

Moreover, if full capital mobility is assumed, the intra-union fixed exchange rate regime makes the policy effect in each country indepent of which member undertakes the operation, as a manifestation of the uniqueness of the money supply for the whole union.

As for the transmission onto the rest of the world, this is absent in the case of a "small" union, defined as unable of affecting rest of the world variables by means of its policy operations. In the case of a "big" union, instead, two hypotheses must be distinguished: if the external exchange rate is flexible, the transmission is negative and works through the responsiveness of the trade balance to changes in the exchange rate, which have, of course, opposite sign in the union and rest of the world; if the exchange rates are fixed, instead, the transmission is positive and works through the redistribution of the change in the supply of money due to the copresence of fixed exchange rates and perfect capital mobility. The results are the same as in the two-country Mundell-Fleming model, since they are worked out on the assumption that the two union member-countries are "mirror images".

The uniqueness of the union money supply imposes, as far as the countries' strategic behaviour is concerned, the necessity for policy coordination, since the system does not have a non-cooperative solution (or a unique non-cooperative solution if the countries are mirror images): this reflects the well known argument that joining an exchange rate union involves the loss of autonomy in the conduction of monetary policy at the national level. If the countries agree to maximize an aggregated objective function, the distribution of the benefits deriving from cooperation depends upon the relative size of the weights attached to each member's utility function: the country of minor economic importance might then doubt the convenience of cooperating if its weight is very small; the same might apply if the members have very different preferences concerning their objective functions targets.

As for macroeconomic policy coordination at the international level, i. e. between the union and the rest of the world, under flexible exchange rates, the transmission being negative, the non-cooperative solution would be too expansionary, but the welfare improving cooperative solution is not sustainable. Moreover, there is no incentive for the countries to act as leaders, since they would be better off as followers and, given the copresence of the intra-union positive and extra-union negative transmission, if the union does not cooperate with the rest of the world, then it is better for its members not to cooperate with each other either, since the negative spillover deriving from the rest of the world and the positive one deriving from the partner tend to offset each other. This contrasts with the argument that a monetary union would be the more viable, the larger its influence on the rest of the world economic variables, and shows how the flexible exchange rate regime calls for less international monetary policy cooperation by its very nature. These results do not apply to the case of a fixed exchange rate regime, characterized by a positive transmission between the union as a whole and the rest of the world as well as between the union members.

As for **fiscal policy**, the transmission from one union member to the other is negative in the short run and in the medium run, since the contractionary effect of the appreciation of the exchange rate towards the rest of the world overcomes the expansion due to the trade linkage mechanisms in the country not undertaking the (expansionary) operation. The overall effect on the union income level depends on the relative sensitivity of money demand in the two members. This is because, given the money stock and the exogenous world interest rate, money demand within the union must remain at the same level as before the fiscal expansion, and therefore the increase in the country undertaking it must equal the contraction in the other one. An expansionary fiscal policy in the country with a higher income sensitivity of money demand, therefore, would cause the union income level to decrease.

The transmission might, instead, be positive in the long run, because of the aggregate supply expansion due to the appreciation, and in the case of a big exchange rate union, since the rest of the world income level and interest rate become endogenous and their increase makes an expansion in both union member-countries compatible with equilibrium in the money market.

The transmission from the union onto the rest of the world is the same as in the two-country Mundell-Fleming model, given the simplifying symmetry assumptions adopted: it is positive under flexible and of uncertain sign under fixed exchange rates.

Cooperation would improve welfare both for the small and the big union. Under flexible exchange rates with the rest of the world, the result that the member countries are better off if they do not cooperate with each other, provided that the union does not cooperate with the rest of the world either, might be obtained, as it was for monetary policy, since the intra-union transmission can be negative and that with the rest of the world is positive, while it could apply under a regime of internationally fixed exchange rates, since in this case the intra-union transmission is positive and that with the rest of the world could be negative.

Which are, then, the effects of the emerging of an exchange rate union on the scope for policy coordination? At the intra-union level, coordination would improve the countries' macroeconomic performance as for the stability of income. However, it is neither necessary, as in the case of monetary policy, since the system would still reach an equilibrium, nor sustainable without the construction of a set of rules on the distribution of benefits and of punishments for the countries which do not stick to the agreed upon solution, since there is no outcome which is both efficient and such that at least one country is not tempted to move away from it. At the international level, the non-cooperative solution would show a contractionary bias under fixed exchange rates and an expansionary one under flexible exchange rates, but the utility improving cooperative and Stackelberg solutions would be unsustainable, and the scope for policy coordination appears to be, therefore, rather limited.

Springer-Verlag and the Environment

We at Springer-Verlag firmly believe that an international science publisher has a special obligation to the environment, and our corporate policies consistently reflect this conviction.

We also expect our business partners – paper mills, printers, packaging manufacturers, etc. – to commit themselves to using environmentally friendly materials and production processes.

The paper in this book is made from low- or no-chlorine pulp and is acid free, in conformance with international standards for paper permanency.

GPSR Compliance

The European Union's (EU) General Product Safety Regulation (GPSR) is a set of rules that requires consumer products to be safe and our obligations to ensure this.

If you have any concerns about our products, you can contact us on ProductSafety@springernature.com

In case Publisher is established outside the EU, the EU authorized representative is:

Springer Nature Customer Service Center GmbH
Europaplatz 3
69115 Heidelberg, Germany

Batch number: 10725973

Printed by Printforce, the Netherlands